Catalysts of the Spirit

An Introduction to Pentecostal History

by

Harry Letson

Bloomington, IN
authorHOUSE®
Milton Keynes, UK

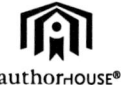

AuthorHouse™
1663 Liberty Drive, Suite 200
Bloomington, IN 47403
www.authorhouse.com
Phone: 1-800-839-8640

AuthorHouse™ UK Ltd.
500 Avebury Boulevard
Central Milton Keynes, MK9 2BE
www.authorhouse.co.uk
Phone: 08001974150

This book is a work of non-fiction. Unless otherwise noted, the author and the publisher make no explicit guarantees as to the accuracy of the information contained in this book and in some cases, names of people and places have been altered to protect their privacy.

© 2007 Harry Letson. All rights reserved.

No part of this book may be reproduced, stored in a retrieval system, or transmitted by any means without the written permission of the author.

First published by AuthorHouse 2/2/2007

ISBN: 978-1-4259-6273-9 (sc)

Printed in the United States of America
Bloomington, Indiana

This book is printed on acid-free paper.

All Scripture and Bible References taken from The Holy Bible, New International Version (1985) New York International Bible Society, New York.

Dedication

To my family for all their help
and support over the years

Contents

Foreword	ix
Preface	xiii
Introduction	1
Chapter 1: Springs of Pentecostalism	16
Chapter 2: W. J. Seymour: Catalyst of Change	39
Chapter 3: T.B. Barratt: Catalyst of Progress	71
Chapter 4: D. J. du Plessis: Catalyst of Unity	94
Conclusion: Pentecostalism - Success or Failure?	116
Bibliography	130

Foreword

Harry Letson is a working Pentecostal pastor in Manchester. He has an earned doctorate for his writing on the life and ministry of another Pentecostal pastor, John Nelson Parr (1886-1976). Nelson Parr was a gifted man who could have made himself a very comfortable living if he had continued in the world of business. Instead he chose to remain as pastor of what became for a time one of the largest Pentecostal churches in Britain. He was a powerful personality, energetic, dedicated and totally committed to winning men and women to Christ. Yet, for all his total commitment to the promotion of the full gospel as proclaimed by his Pentecostal convictions, it was in his preaching that Parr made his chief contribution. The fruits of this work were clearly seen in the growth of his "Bethshan" assembly in Longsight, Manchester. This was also evident in the lives of the numbers of young men and women who were led to Christ through his ministry and who subsequently pastored churches.

It is this focus on the priority of preaching among Pentecostals that the author is concerned with. There are a good number of books available today that tell the story of some of the pioneers of Pentecostalism (with the focus of attention being largely on the United States). This is understandable, particularly in view of the celebration of the centenary of the outpouring of the Holy Spirit in April 1906 in Los Angeles. Much of the attention has naturally focused upon the distinctive emphasis on speaking in tongues as evidence of the baptism of the Holy Spirit.

The Pentecostal Movement as it was to become known was to become much more than "The Tongues Movement." It was described as such by some of its early critics as well as a lesser number in later years (who ought to have known better).

At the beginning there were only a few converts in Azusa Street. Many of the early visitors were Christian workers who looked to God to "give the same gift to them."(Acts 11: 17) Many were to receive. Within a short time many of them, instead of staying on to indulge themselves in the euphoria of their newfound experience went from there to proclaim by preaching, not only in the surrounding areas but to the remoter corners of the earth.

It is this work Dr Letson focuses attention to the importance of preaching within early Pentecostalism and he looks at some of the figures that made an important contribution to its formation.

Pentecostal preaching was "different." Whether it was an African-American such as Seymour or the English-born Norwegian, Thomas Ball Barratt to sometimes almost conversational style of others. I know that for myself it was this preaching that brought me to Christ following the challenge of the first sermon I ever heard in the first Pentecostal church I entered when I was seventeen years of age.

There are many different styles of preaching, even in Pentecostalism. If this book will encourage one person to look again at their preaching and to give it a higher priority it will have served its purpose.

Desmond Cartwright

Cardiff

Introduction

Ministers are servants of God, set in place to work out his purposes in the world around them. Each one has his or her own philosophy of ministry enshrined within the specific 'models of ministry' they each espouse.[4] Since the inception of Christianity on the Day of Pentecost" (Acts 2:1) God has been speaking to this world and manifesting his presence by his Spirit through the ministry of his church and particularly its leaders. In this sense leaders become catalysts of the Spirit within the context of ministry. So how can we define the ministry of the church and its leaders and the changes which have occurred in it? If it has changed what are they and where does the Pentecostal Church fit into it all? It would be helpful, as a starting point, to define briefly what ministry means in general with the aid of certain models and endeavour to build one for the Pentecostal Church.

The Traditional View. For most people the common concept of ministry is that of a separated clergy aloof from the laity or common people. They are seen as trained professionals set apart from the rest of the church membership. For Gordon Fee this model developed over the centuries to find "...its sharpest expression in the Roman Catholic communion, but finding its way into almost every form of Protestantism as well." [5]

The Modified View. Not everyone accepted the hierarchical or professional concept of ministry. Many down through the years emphasised the church as a brotherhood with its leadership emerging from among the people. They practised a simple lifestyle as a brotherhood of believers with no professional paid ministry or priesthood. It was out of this non-professional dimension of ministry that Pentecostalism was born. Indeed, many of these early pioneers almost took an anti-professional stance in rejecting any form of paid ministry. The real driving force of Pentecostalism then is its view of ministry. In one sense Pentecostals see themselves as the true successors of primitive New Testament Christianity. It sought to return power to people in the pews not to priests in the parish or preachers in the pulpit. A Pentecostal theology" of ministry then must have this as its foundation and focus - power to the people! Leadership in the church, according to Pentecostalism, should be there to serve and facilitate the empowerment of God's people.

The Pentecostal Ministry

Essentially, the Pentecostal view of ministry is an inclusive one. It sees all God's people as potential instruments of power. Peter declared on the Day of Pentecost: *"In the last days God says I will pour out my Spirit on all people. Your sons and daughters will prophesy, your young men will see visions, your old men will dream dreams."* (Acts 2: 17 and Joel 2:28.) According to Pentecostals the Holy Spirit has now come to empower and equip all God's people not merely an isolated few for some specific ministry. Gordon D. Fee calls it *The Empowering Presence of God* - the title of his book.[6]

The Pentecostal View. This includes the centrality of the work of the Holy Spirit and how He empowers and equips leadership for the specific task of equipping the church to reach the world with the Gospel and the presence of God. Pentecostal ministry is about releasing people into ministry and gifting by the power of the Spirit. It is very much in line with, what Fee calls, "The Biblical Leadership Model" and less in line with the "Contemporary Ecclesiastical Structure" of the church.

The task in this work is to examine and explore the rise and development, history and influence of the Pentecostal ministry in the twentieth century. This will be done by examining the environment in which Pentecostalism was born and showing how it was manifested in the lives and works of certain individual ministers – the catalysts of the Spirit.

Pentecostalism has become the third force in Christianity today according to Lesslie Newbigin's book *The Household of God*. In it he aligns Pentecostalism with the other two great Christian movements - Catholicism and Protestantism. Newbigin argues that whereas Catholicism provides order through its liturgy and Protestantism faith based on rational thinking; Pentecostalism emphasises experience. [7] James Dunn adds another strand to this saying: "In fact, it represents a fourth major strand in Christianity - alongside Orthodoxy, Roman Catholicism and Protestantism." [8] Pentecostalism then is a force to be reckoned within the world. But what brought it about?

Pentecostal Dynamics

In his book: *Where Do We Go from Here?* Ralph Neighbour" states: "Theology breeds methodology...."[9] In other words nothing happens in a vacuum. Just as politics needs an ideology to fuel it and impel it forward, so the Christian ministry needs theology to make it effective. The Pentecostal ministry is no different. At a joint Conference of Elim and Assemblies of God in Bognor Regis (April 1997) Colin Dye of Kensington Temple, London, said that unlike the term charismatic, Pentecostal was a doctrinal statement. He added that many in the historic churches had brought the Pentecostal experience of the Holy Spirit into their fellowships but their beliefs and practices have remained unchanged. For Dye, to be Pentecostal meant to embrace all the doctrinal beliefs and theology associated with it. What are these beliefs and practices and how have they affected the Pentecostal ministry down through the years?

There was a time when the concept of Pentecostals having any kind of theology was a joke. At its inception Pentecostals were seen at best as shallow and frivolous and at worst sinister and dangerous. Pentecostals, it seemed, were more interested in experience than doctrine. Such bad press must be viewed sceptically as it came from critics outside the movement who judged the early revival in very negative terms without due regard to what Pentecostalism was about. However, a glance at some of the early Pentecostal magazines such as *Redemption Tidings* and the *Elim Evangel* would have put paid to the misnomer of Pentecostalism's lack of theology. Some of the blame, in the early days, could be laid at the door of Pentecostals themselves due to their anti-intellectual stance which critics wrongly considered a lack of thought and theological reflection. Things, though, have moved on apace in the last few decades with most of the Pentecostal fellowships in America and Europe having their own theological colleges which provide degree programmes for their prospective ministers.

Pentecostals have always aligned themselves theologically with orthodox Protestantism. Their emphasis on the trustworthiness of scripture and justification by faith has been at the crux of their message from the beginning and remains so. However, the real hallmark of their theological emphasis is their desire to get back to the New Testament model of the church and its ministry. This too was the objective of the Reformers of course. Pentecostals assert that they have restored New Testament beliefs, practices and experiences to the church. This is confirmed by David A. Womack in the preface of his book on the writings of Donald Gee.[10] He says: "We now use the word *Pentecostal* (author's italics) to mean the concept that there is one true Christianity that was taught by Jesus Christ and His followers...Pentecostals identify themselves with the beliefs, experiences, practices and priorities of original, apostolic, New Testament Christianity." This may sound a rather pretentious claim in this age of greater ecumenical

Catalysts of the Spirit

engagement but for Womack, like Colin Dye, Charismatic only refers to one aspect of Pentecostal experience - the gifts of the Holy Spirit. We need then to explore the theological underpinnings of Pentecostal beliefs and practices within the context of early Pentecostals and what they called the Foursquare Gospel.

The Foursquare Gospel [11]

The orthodoxy of Pentecostalism is best expressed in Aimee Semple McPherson's "Foursquare Gospel of Jesus Christ as Saviour, Healer, Baptiser and Coming King",[12] though this was not original to McPherson as Malcolm Hathaway points out. It also encapsulates the distinctive differences in the Pentecostal movement from other fellowships as evidenced in the outworking of its ministry such as healing and the baptism of the Holy Spirit. Gee, however, warns of the danger of the overuse of this "slogan" as ".... it may become mechanical as a phrase, and stultify evangelical preaching and testimony into the one fixed rut of expression."[13] Notwithstanding, let us discover these 'distinctives' in Pentecostal ministry.

Saviour. The preaching of the evangelical gospel has been of paramount importance to Pentecostals particularly the early pioneers who stressed evangelism as a response to the outpouring of the gifts of the Spirit. The miraculous and the baptism in the Spirit were only a means to an end. They were never intended as ends in themselves. Early Pentecostals saw themselves as the legitimate heirs of the great revivalists of bygone ages. What they had was not a new gospel but a fuller one. These early Pentecostals stood firm on the Reformation principle of justification by faith. In this they followed such people as the Wesleys, Whitefield, Finney, Moody and others who sought to bring people to a personal experience of faith.[14]

Healer. Alongside its emphasis on instantaneous conversion, Pentecostal theology stresses the possibility of healing the sick. Pentecostals of course were not the first to talk and write about these things; the healing message had been around for some time before the emergence of Pentecostalism. What was different about the Pentecostal emphasis, and Assemblies of God in particular, was the added doctrine of healing in the atonement. That is that Jesus died to provide healing for believers as well as salvation. The next chapter deals somewhat with this aspect of Pentecostalism and its origins so comments on healing will be reserved for then.[15]

Baptiser. This is in reference to the doctrine referred to as the baptism of the Holy Spirit. This is a specific reference to the experience of the early church in Acts 2 when the church was filled with the Holy Spirit. The occurrence happened on the Day of Pentecost and it is from this Pentecostals derive their name. The term baptism in the Spirit recalls the promise made by John the Baptist in Matthew 3:11:

> I baptise you with water for repentance. But after me will come one who is more powerful than I, whose sandals I am not fit to carry. He will baptise you with the Holy Spirit and with fire. (See also: Mark 1:8; Luke 3:16; Acts 11:16)

The baptism in the Spirit then is seen as an enduement of power for Christian service in that those who receive it are filled with the Spirit to overflowing. This is distinct from conversion. Once again this was not new in itself as many of the holiness groups had been teaching this 'second blessing' since the time of the Moravians and the Wesleys. What was different about Pentecostals, on the whole, is their insistence on evidentiary tongues which they called 'the initial evidence'. For Pentecostals, this experience enabled a Christian to exercise the supernatural gifts of the Spirit.[16]

Coming King. A strong, recurring theme in Pentecostal preaching and worship was the soon coming of Christ.

This too had a distinctive characteristic particularly in early Pentecostalism in that it was dominated by Dispensationalism. More will be said of this also in the next chapter but suffice it to say it is a theological system which divides the whole of human history into seven distinct periods of time and lays great emphasis on Israel with the promises of God to be fulfilled to them as a people.[17] This was the distinctive feature of Brethrenism and the teaching of John Nelson Darby in particular. The emphasis was on the imminent return of Christ and the secret rapture in which all those who had come to faith in Christ between the death of Christ and 'the rapture' would be caught up to meet the Lord in the air.

It was these theological distinctives then which gave early Pentecostals their evangelistic thrust, driving them on to bring as many to faith before Christ would come for the church in the secret rapture. This latter day urgency was fuelled by the manifestation of revival and supernatural gifts which Pentecostals saw as a definite sign of the imminent return of Christ.

Yet these distinctives also fed into other aspects of activity namely the way they operated in public and the local church. This could be called Pentecostal praxis or their accepted practices and customs.

Pentecostal Praxis

How all these things are worked out in practice is what Pentecostal ministry is about and, in many ways that is what this work is seeking to demonstrate. The foregoing is a simple prelude to all that follows in the life and ministry of each of the noted characters being dealt with in this work, but what kind of things did they do which may have been somewhat different from other ministries?

Ministry This has to do with leadership and its public face. The way that early Pentecostal leaders have presented and engaged others in the tenets of their faith has become unique in itself. Although they had much in common with holiness and revivalist preachers in outreach, Pentecostals added their own brand of style. Zeal, enthusiasm, excitement and passion characterised most Pentecostal ministry and services in preaching and worship. There was, literally, a 'hands on' approach in that they exercised the laying on of hands for healing and blessing as well as anointing with oil. Frequent appeals and altar calls at the end of the services for salvation, restoration of backsliders and healing were common.

So the Pentecostal praxis of ministry was to take it to the people and evoke a response from them to receive from God there and then whatever they may need in salvation, healing, filling with the Spirit, guidance or even deliverance from demons. The practical application of theology to the individual is what Pentecostalism was looking for.

Service. Not only were Pentecostals striving to make God's promises freely available to all who needed them, they were also seeking to release God's people to function within the local church and the body of Christ with gifting and ability. Challenging people to be filled with the Spirit and to launch out in the gifts of the Spirit and evangelism were common features of many Pentecostal meetings. Good Pentecostal leadership was perceived as that which motivated God's people to service within the body of Christ.

This praxis of service can be seen then as an extension of Pentecostal ministry itself. Early Pentecostals were not so concerned with being pew fillers but instruments of God utilised by the Holy Spirit.

Outreach. Evangelism and reaching out to those considered as lost are at the heart of Pentecostalism today. This was so in the early days and Pentecostals would claim this is still true to day. This is undoubtedly true but the difference between now and the early days is a difference in emphasis. In the early days mass evangelism and great public gatherings were the order of the day.

Catalysts of the Spirit

Pentecostal evangelists such as Aimee Semple McPherson projected Pentecostalism into the forefront of religious life in America. In Britain Smith Wigglesworth and the Jeffreys brothers also did much to highlight the evangelistic thrust of the fledgling movement as well. This tended to strengthen the perception of Pentecostalism's evangelistic impetus, yet it may have overshadowed the efforts of ordinary ministers on the ground doing exceptional work without being recognised. That is men like John Nelson Parr in Manchester whose church became, arguably, the largest Pentecostal church in Britain before WWII within the Assemblies of God fold.[18] Percy Brewster of the British Elim Church is another as well as T.B. Barrett in Oslo, Norway and Lewi Petrus in Stockholm, Sweden to mention a few.

If time and space permitted it we could mention numerous other ministers and missionaries who risked life and limb at great cost and sacrifice to bring the Pentecostal message to the world. Mention could also be made at this point of the social dimension of Pentecostalism but this will be dealt with in another chapter. Robert Anderson highlights this too in his work on the making of Pentecostalism in America,[19] as does Douglas Petersen in his work on social concern in South America.[20]

Harry Letson

Having sought to outline the rationale behind the work and lay a few preliminary foundations we are now ready to look at the history of Pentecostal ministry and its influence on the world at large. The next chapter will seek to plot the course of Pentecostalism in a historical and theological context before looking at the individuals who could, arguably, be said to be the founding fathers of the Pentecostal movement.

---

[4] Ian Bunting has written a useful little book in the Grove Series of Books entitled: *Models of Ministry: Managing the Church Today*, Grove Books Ltd, Cambridge, (1993, 1996)

[5] Fee, *Gospel and Spirit* p122 Also, see this book for models of the Traditional and Modified forms of ministry.

[6] G.D. Fee, (1994, 3rd print 1995) *The Empowering Presence of God: The Holy Spirit in the Letters of Paul* Hendrickson Publishers, Inc Peabody, Mass. U.S.A.

[7] Lesslie Newbegin, (1954) *The Household of God* Friendship Press, New York. According to Richard Massey, Donald Gee commented on this in the June 1965 edition of *Pentecost,* Richard Massey (1992), *Another Springtime - Donald Gee: Pentecostal Pioneer,* Highland Books, Guildford, Surrey, Massey reproduces it intact in his book p148-151

[8] James Dunn, "*Pentecostals and Charismatics*" Lion PC History of Christianity, Lion PC Handbook (1993, 1994)

[9] R. W. Neighbour, (1990) *Where Do We Go From Here?* Touch Publications, Houston. Texas. USA p93

[10] David A. Womack, Compiler and Editor (1998), *Pentecostal Experience: The Writings of Donald Gee* Gospel Publishing House, Springfield, Missouri. USA p13

[11] Malcolm R. Hathaway, "The Elim Pentecostal Church: Origins, Development and Distinctive" *Pentecostal Perspectives,* Keith Warrington, (Ed) (1998) Paternoster Press, Carlisle. England. p6

[12] Donald Gee (1941) *The Pentecostal Movement,* Victory Press, London, England. p122

[13] ibid

[14] Gee, *The Pentecostal Movement* p6

[15] Keith Warrington, "Healing and Exorcism: The Path to Wholeness" *Pentecostal Perspectives,* Keith Warrington ,(Ed) (1998) Paternoster Press, Carlisle. Section 7

[16] David Petts, "The Baptism in the Holy Spirit: The Theological Distinctive" *Pentecostal Perspectives,* Keith Warrington (Ed) (1998) Paternoster Press, Carlisle. Section 5

[17] James J. Glass, "Eschatology: A Clear and Present Danger – A Sure and Certain Hope" (1998), *Pentecostal Perspectives,* Keith Warrington (Ed) Paternoster Press, Carlisle. Section 6

[18] Henry Letson, (2005) *Keeper of the Flame: The Story of John Nelson Parr,* unpublished PhD Thesis, University of Wales, Bangor.

[19] Robert M. Anderson, (1979), *Vision of the Disinherited: The Making of American Pentecostalism,* Oxford University Press, Oxford and New York

[20] D. Petersen, (1996) *Not by Might Nor By Power: A Pentecostal Theology of Social Concern in Latin America.* Regnum Books International, Paternoster Press, Carlisle England.

Chapter 1: Springs of Pentecostalism

A favourite term of Pentecostals for their church and its development is not a denomination but a "movement".[21] This is so because early Pentecostals were greatly averse to organisation and institutionalisation preferring to see what was happening as a great move of God upon his people everywhere. Many also refer to it as a stream or river which also implies movement - an ever-flowing stream[22] meandering its way down the course of time and the history of the Church, affecting people in every generation. Indeed, most early Pentecostals refer to Pentecostal phenomena at various junctures of church history. Donald Gee and T.B. Barratt[23] give examples of this. In this sense Pentecostalism, to early Pentecostals, was part and parcel of historic Christianity and in the vanguard of all the plans and purposes of God for his world in their day and generation. What then were the historic springs and tributaries which flowed together to form the modern religious phenomena known as Pentecostalism?

Catalysts of the Spirit

At least five strands of Christian tradition are observable in the Pentecostal movement and ministry. Each has made a significant contribution to the rich tapestry of Pentecostal life and service. They are the Evangelical Faith, the Revivalist Element, the Holiness Movements, the Healing Phenomena and the Brethren Impact.

The Evangelical Faith It is from the Reformation, with its emphasis on returning to New Testament Christianity and the Word of God, that Pentecostals get their evangelicalism. They preach firmly, with evangelistic fervour, the Reformation theology of justification by faith. Unlike the Reformers, however, Pentecostal preachers tend to favour Arminianism with its emphasis on human responsibility [24] along with the basic Reformed tradition of the necessity of the Atonement of Christ and the application of salvation to the heart of penitent sinners. There is some affinity too with the Puritans and their emphasis on purifying the church of all worldly practices, the simplification of worship and greater involvement by the laity as well as the experience of salvation in the life of the believer. The experiential Christianity of the Puritans is well documented. Ian Breward says of Puritan theologians: "These preacher-theologians wrote in detail about the way God's grace could be identified in human experience...." He goes on to say: "...their emphases on religious experience and practical piety gave their writings an accent which was unusual among Reformed theologians...." [25]

Traditionally then Pentecostals have placed themselves within the Protestant tradition with their emphasis on the need of salvation as an individual experience.

The Revivalist Element The revivalist element, and preaching to the masses, was introduced into the Christian ministry by the Wesley brothers and George Whitefield. John Wesley, according to Gerald Parsons, was a strange mixture of revivalist and churchman. To Parsons he was "...both an emotional and fervent revivalist and a clerical autocrat."[26] Another important figure in the development of revivalist thinking was Jonathan Edwards. Edwards was involved in what has come to be known as "The Great Awakening" between 1734-35 and again 1740-1742. The second of these periods is associated with George Whitefield.[27] Edwards reflected on these occurrences in some of his books, notably *A Narrative of Surprising Conversions* first published in 1736.[28] Edwards is reputed to be one of America's finest philosopher-theologians who applied all his faculties to understand revival. Later American evangelists such as James Caughey in the 1840s and C.G. Finney in 1859-1862 built on the work of Wesley, Whitefield and Edwards. Phoebe Palmer in the 1860s and D.L. Moody in 1873-1874 took it even further.[29]

Mass evangelism and revivalism were very much in place by the time Pentecostalism came on the scene. These two elements have always been at the heart of Pentecostal activity and many of the early pioneers helped to promote the message of Pentecost through the medium of mass gatherings.

The Holiness Movements [30] The Pentecostal Movement of today undoubtedly sprung out of the Holiness movements of the 18th and 19th Centuries. Men like John Wesley, with his stress on Christian Perfectionism or entire sanctification, began the new drive for holiness as a second work of grace. The evidence of this 'second blessing' was variously described in relational terms such as Wesley's perfect love, manifested as spiritual experiences of joy and peace. In time this led to a re-defining of Wesleyan 'Perfectionism' in Britain and America. Some stayed with traditional Wesleyanism whilst others modified it, such as the Keswick Convention,[31] which eventually moved away from the Methodist tradition of eradication of sin to a suspension of it.[32] That is, not the total removal of sin from the believer but to be so close to God as to suspend its effects.

In America the emphasis on holiness as a movement was given great impetus by the upsurge of the National Camp

Meeting Association for the Promotion of Holiness in 1867. This brought the leaders of the Camp Meeting Association into conflict with the Methodist leadership who saw them as dangerous extremists, which in some ways they were. In America the Association began to spawn, unintentionally, a number of independent Holiness churches. These came to be viewed as holding extreme views on church order, which, to the more established leaders, appeared to lack discipline. The emphasis, as with most Holiness Churches, was that sanctification was a second and subsequent experience to salvation and even a third stage in some cases.

Charles Finney often spoke of 'perfectionism' as a definite, instantaneous experience. His book *Power from on High*[33] is actually a collection of articles by him on the Spirit-filled life. In this book he specifically refers to this power as "The baptism of the Holy Spirit". However, one of the first people to popularise the message was Phoebe Palmer[34] although Gee suggests Dr Torrey should be credited with elucidating it doctrinally.[35] Canon John Gunstone, former Anglican Ecumenical Officer of Manchester, however, has another interesting perspective on this. Gunstone introduces a new name into the current debate saying the phrase can be traced back to Symeon the New Theologian (949-1022).[36] However, it is the influences on the Pentecostal movement, prior to its emergence, we are seeking to establish.

Not everyone was comfortable with the Wesleyan definition of holiness and sanctification. One such theologian was W.E. Boardman. He was from a Reformed background, the American Presbyterian Church. He rejected Wesleyan Perfectionism but advocated a second experience of grace clearly distinct from justification. His ideas were expressed in his book *The Higher Christian Life* (1859).[37] This book gained great popularity and influenced such people as Robert and Hanna Pearsall-Smith. The Pearsall-Smiths added their own brand of holiness to Boardman's understanding of the issue. It was this Higher-Life Theology more than Wesleyan Holiness, which affected a change in the Holiness tradition in Britain. It eventually flowered in the renowned Keswick Convention of 1875.[38] It was this later type of holiness teaching rather than Wesleyan holiness, which early British Pentecostals latched on to. The emphasis was on power for living the Christian life, which was received by faith.

Wesleyanism and revivalism also introduced another element, which came forth with great power from Holiness groups. The element is that of music, praise and worship.

From Charles Wesley to Ira D. Sankey one of the lasting contributions to the Pentecostal movement by holiness and revivalist groups is music and singing.[39] The other was the emphasis on healing.

The Healing Phenomenon Healing the sick has always had a firm basis in Christian theology but it was its association with the Holiness movements, particularly in America, which gave it its modern renown. People like A.J. Gordon, A.B. Simpson and R. Kelso Carter in America laid a strong foundation for it through the holiness movement and particularly Carter's emphasis on healing in the atonement. W. E. Boardman also led the way with his International Conference on Divine Healing and True Holiness in London, England in 1885. Together with Mrs Baxter and Mrs Murray he founded the first faith home in Britain in 1882 - a centre for healing in London known as Bethshan. The healing phenomenon was given a further boost also by Andrew Murray. This influential South African minister claims to have personally experienced a miraculous cure and from that time on promoted it in his book *Divine Healing.*

One of the most influential, though controversial characters in the area of divine healing was John Alexander Dowie.[40] Dowie was drawn to the concept of divine healing as a result of an epidemic in 1876 during his pastorate in Newtown, Sydney, Australia. It is said that as a result of praying for the sick and seeing successful results he stemmed the tide of deaths in Newtown. His success in Australia led him to believe he should emigrate to America. He did so with his wife in 1888. He established his own community, Zion City Illinois, and his own Christian Catholic Church. Dowie's subsequent impact on Pentecostalism was very significant indeed.[41]

Another person of great influence in advancing the cause of divine healing was Charles Cullis. He was a Boston doctor who promoted the doctrine of divine healing through his Faith Conventions. David Allen claims that it was chiefly through Cullis that the healing movement eventually converged with the holiness movement.[42] Two others who laid the foundation for the doctrine of Healing in the Atonement as expressed in Pentecostalism were R.L. Stanton in his *Gospel Parallelisms: Illustrated in the Healing of the Body and Soul* (1883) and R. Kelso Carter's *The Atonement of Sin and Sickness or A Full Salvation for Soul and Body* (1884). So by the time Pentecostalism arrived on the scene in the early twentieth century healing had become an established tenet of faith in a number of holiness and revivalist groups.

The Brethren Impact The Brethren movement and particularly those associated with John Nelson Darby, has had a profound and enduring effect on Pentecostalism since its inception. Ian Randall says it was "A crucial factor in shaping Pentecostalism...."[43] Randall argues that the Brethren's concept of "...restoring New Testament church life" contributed to the rise of Pentecostalism. This Brethren contribution to Pentecostalism and the Charismatic Movement[44] expressed itself chiefly in two ways - in ecclesiology and eschatology.

Ecclesiology Randall claims that early Pentecostal meetings were based largely on the Brethren format of service. Communion or 'breaking of bread' were weekly occurrences at which they often sat in a circle around the communion table. Some even sang from the Brethren hymnbook. The Brethren also emphasised the importance of being led by and waiting upon the Spirit for inspiration. They baptised believers by immersion and spoke about spiritual gifts, though not in the Pentecostal sense it has to be said.[45] The Brethren concept of tithing, or giving one tenth of one's income to the church, was also taken over by Pentecostal churches. In time, too, the 'sectarian' or exclusive emphasis was gradually adopted by many Pentecostal groups and denominations. Early Pentecostals also used Brethren terms and phrases such as 'assembly', 'the saints' (referring to the people of God) and referred to one another as brother and sister. Many Pentecostal ministers acknowledge their Brethren background.

These early meetings then probably looked and behaved more like Brethren meetings apart from the greater freedom and general participation of all its members. In short, as Randall puts it, "Brethren customs and priorities helped to shape the Pentecostal ethos."[46]

Eschatology During the nineteenth century many Adventist and Millenarian groups emerged due to the rising interest in prophecy and the Second Coming. Many of them were generally regarded as heretical, like Jehovah's Witnesses, Seventh Day Adventists, Christadelphians and Mormons, though Mormons may be less eschatological than most. The eschatological interest in the nineteenth century fed into the emerging Pentecostal psyche. Douglas Petersen elucidates this for us showing how J.N. Darby influenced Keswick in Britain with his Dispensational system of theology and then went on to influence many holiness leaders in America and names some of them.[47] The development of modern Dispensationalism, with its emphasis on a secret rapture, was just the kind of theological framework the budding Pentecostals were looking for.[48] Most Pentecostal pioneers were thoroughly Pre-millennial due to the influence of Darby on the Holiness movement. This was strange as many Dispensationalists were cessationists.[49] Most scholars acknowledge that the early Pentecostals associated the outpouring of the Spirit in the twentieth century with the Second Coming of Christ and Darby's emphasis on the imminent return of Christ supremely fitted the bill. D. William Faupel, for example, sees the Pentecostal movement as a Millenarian one,[50] but within the context of Darby's Dispensational teaching.[51] John F. Walvoord argues that "...the dispensational idea is as old as theology itself, with elaborate dispensational systems being evolved even before Christ."[52] Yet Philip Mauro (1859-1952) contends that it was Malachi Taylor of the American Brethren, who gave modern Dispensationalism its distinctively Jewish character.[53] Added to all this was the publication of the Scofield Reference Bible in 1909 and its specific brand of Dispensationalism. It was Dispensationalism, with its emphasis on literal biblical interpretation, which filtered its way through to Pentecostal theology. Dispensational Pre-millennialism, its literalism and the secret rapture, come out very clearly in the writings of early Pentecostals and their Statements of Faith.[54]

Some scholars though argue for a more sociological understanding of the rise of Pentecostalism within the context of the American social milieu of industrialisation, urbanisation and the emergence of third world countries.[55] However, the hardships encountered by Pentecostals during these early days may have made the concept of an imminent return of Christ very appealing indeed.

Brethrenism, then, made a great impact on Pentecostal life and practices as did evangelical Protestantism in general, along with the various Holiness groups and teaching on healing.[56] In many ways Brethrenism provided the cohesion of a biblical framework of ecclesiology and eschatology for Pentecostalism and helped to propel it forward into the twentieth century.

The Pentecostal Phenomenon

D. William Faupel uses the imagery of conception and birth in order to understand and explain the significance of the Pentecostal phenomena. He says: "When the child is born, it will have the features of both parents."[57] In this sense Pentecostalism bears all the theological and ecclesiological traits of its forebears as outlined above. These traits became pronounced and manifested particularly in its ministry. So what is Pentecostalism and how did these various strands of Christian tradition find expression in Pentecostal life and ministry? What is it about Pentecostalism that has made it the force it is in today's world? Perhaps the best way to answer this question is to see it in three distinct forms - Its Characteristics, Its Message and Its Achievement.

Its Characteristics. To most people the one thing which characterises a Pentecostal meeting is its liveliness or to some its overt emotionalism. The singing is enthusiastic, charismata or gifts of the Spirit are often in operation - tongues, interpretation, prophecy - and given with emotional force; preachers sometimes shout or cry. The preaching is often fiery and pointed and it usually ends with an appeal for prayer. During such prayer emotional displays are also common. People may cry or laugh or fall down. Many claim great blessing and confess healings or some other sort of miracle. Bloch-Hoell confirms this saying: "In a Pentecostal assembly it is considered quite acceptable to show one's feelings."[58] He goes on to explain them as ecstatic experiences saying they are: "...ecstatic manifestations...visions, motoric movement (glossolalia), and loss of consciousness." To Pentecostals such activity is more than mere ecstasy; it is the manifestation of the presence of God by his Spirit. Bloch-Hoell is right though in saying Pentecostals react against the formalism of institutionalised Christianity but they would not accept his calling these reactions "...primitive emotions...."[59]

Catalysts of the Spirit

Pentecostals are adamant in their desire to see God manifested in their presence by signs, wonders and miracles. They take scripture literally and believe it to be applicable for today. They also have a wholehearted desire to see the world evangelised and believe such manifestations aid the evangelisation of the world.

Much of this excitement and emotionalism comes from the revivalist and holiness tradition which affirmed emotional experiences. The music, the singing, the enthusiasm and the joy were also typical of revivalist and holiness meetings. In this way Pentecostalism inherited its characteristics from its spiritual forebears, adding its own emphasis on the miraculous as a sign of the presence of God among his people and as a sign of the imminent return of Christ which would aid evangelism.

Its Message. The means of achieving this evangelism is mainly through its message. The most succinct definition of its message was that defined by Aimee Semple McPherson - The Foursquare Gospel of Jesus Christ as Saviour, Healer, Baptiser in the Holy Spirit and Coming King. It encapsulates what Pentecostals call: "The Full Gospel". This too has come down to Pentecostals from its predecessors in the various traditions. Faupel amplifies this by showing the "...five cardinal points...."[60] of

Pentecostalism. He draws on Donald Dayton's "...'gestalt' of five characteristics of Pentecostal themes: justification, sanctification, divine healing, the second coming of Christ and the baptism of the Holy Spirit."[61] Faupel continues by showing Dayton's "...inner logic of the message...."[62] in the four common names used by Pentecostals. They are "Full Gospel, Latter Rain, Apostolic and Pentecostal." The first one - the Full Gospel - Faupel says relates to the five-fold pattern already mentioned whilst "The other three provide the infrastructure which gave the message its dynamic coherence."[63]

Pentecostalism in its ministry to the church and the world sees itself as a fuller expression of the gospel of Christ. It conveys a message which shows its concern for the whole person - body, soul and spirit; a message with a highly individualistic appeal. In other words, God is here to meet every individual need - spiritually, physically, emotionally, psychologically and, in recent years, financially as well.

Many Pentecostals are now seeking to move away from the "other-worldly", individualistic emphasis to a more social dimension in their theology and practice; an "orthopraxis" perhaps which, according to Faupel, is about "...right living as well as correct belief."[64]

Its Achievements Every aspect of Christian life has been affected by the Pentecostal phenomenon in one form or another. It has drawn criticism and praise from all sections of the church. It has been accused of demonism, manipulation and heresy. Yet it has influenced, forever, the shape and form of church life and theology whether one agrees with it or not. It has also shown itself to be at the forefront of social action in spite of its "other-worldly" eschatological emphasis.

Social Achievements Douglas Petersen shows that recent studies have called these "other-worldly"[65] criticisms of Pentecostalism into question. He says: "Increasingly, Pentecostalism is now viewed as an initiative expressed in religious form by aspiring but disadvantaged social individuals and groups."[66] Petersen seems to be arguing that it was the poor social conditions of these early Pentecostals, as much as any spiritual considerations that prompted the emergence of Pentecostalism. This is because its first pioneers had a social dimension to their vision and theology, as we will see. It was a vision, which embraced all races, classes, creeds and colours. In this sense it has been successful in causing the church to rethink itself and the place of the so-called 'laity' within its walls. It has also brought the whole question of gender to the fore in not only permitting women to exercise gifts of the Spirit but to function in ministry as well. However, it has to be said that Pentecostalism, like the Church as a whole, may have lost its way somewhat in these things and God has had to restore it again and again. In recent years Pentecostal groups may have become more interested in establishing their own denominational enclaves than reviving and unifying the church as a whole. Others have added to this the maintaining of white, male supremacy rather than true equality, though this is hotly debated by recent scholarship. If this is so perhaps this is why new movements arise from time to time, to quicken and refresh the church by the Holy Spirit working among them.

Theological Achievements Although many of the first Pentecostals were uneducated and untrained as theologians they had a perception of God and society which brought a freshness to their Christian experience, a point adequately made by Bloch-Hoell in his work on the Pentecostal movement. He quotes from the Minutes of the 41st Annual Assembly of the Church of God (Cleveland) saying: "The greater percentage of these men were poor and from humble walks of life. Many were labourers and farmers with limited education...." He goes on to say: "The Pentecostal Movement still lacks university-trained ministers, scholarly theology, liturgical tradition, Church art...."[67] It may be true that early Pentecostal pioneers were very distrustful of seats of learning which they felt endangered their faith or undermined their confidence in God and his Word, but many of them had great insight into aspects of the bible and theology. This mistrust still exists in many quarters today in Pentecostal churches. Indeed, early Pentecostals seemed more against liberal Protestantism than liturgical Christianity; they saw liberalism as creeping paralysis in the church. This anti-intellectualism may not have been due so much to the lack of education, as a mistrust of institutionalism and formalism which they felt would hinder and stultify the work of the Holy Spirit in the church. Bloech-Hoell's statement may have been true in 1964, when the work was published, but things have moved on apace since then. Pentecostalism has become much more self-confident and educated in the intervening years and with the upsurge of degree programmes in many Pentecostal colleges, particularly in America and recently in Britain, things are changing. Pentecostal theological journals are also a hopeful sign of greater theological reflection by the Pentecostal movement.

Spiritual Achievements The spiritual contribution of Pentecostalism to the universal church is generally acknowledged. It has brought freshness to our experience of God and increased joyfulness in worship. New churches and denominations have been formed and older churches and denominations have been revived. Individuals testify to having received salvation, forgiveness of sins and a changed life whilst others claim physical, psychological and emotional healing. Foreign missions have also been greatly enhanced. The work of the Spirit too is discussed in churches, universities and even in the media as never before.

It all came about through the Pentecostal revival at the turn of the twentieth century in an old converted stable in Azusa Street in Los Angeles. The place of Azusa Street to the origins of Pentecostalism and its ministry is now generally acknowledged.[68] Scotland also quotes Frank Bartleman as saying: "Few events have affected modern history as greatly as the famous Azusa Street revival 1906-1909 which ushered into being the worldwide twentieth century revival."[69]

This revival and Azusa Street's place in it will be examined in the next three chapters through the ministries of three men - W.J. Seymour, T.B. Barratt and David J. du Plessis. The contribution of these men to the founding and expansion of Pentecostalism throughout the world is immense. Each in his own way is rightly seen as a spiritual catalyst for his time. In this context many people, both men and woman, have acted in this capacity but for the sake of time and space we will concentrate on the three mentioned above.

---

[21] Donald Gee uses it as the title of his book, *The Pentecostal Movement* Victory Press, London (1941) as does Nils Bloch-Hoell in his influential work: *The Pentecostal Movement: It Origin, Development and Distinctive Character* Universtetforlaget, Oslo and Allen and Unwin London (1964)
[22] David Allen uses this imagery in his book *The Unfailing Stream* Sovereign World, Tonbridge, England (1994)
[23] Gee, *The Pentecostal Movement* p2,3 and T.B. Barratt (1909 reprinted 1928) *In The Days of the Latter Rain* Elim Publishing Co Ltd. Ch 3 "Tongues of Fire"
[24] J.W. Ward describes it as "...one stream within Arminian evangelicalism...." *The New Dictionary of Theology* Editors Sinclair B. Ferguson and David F. Wright, (1988) Inter-Varsity Press, Leicester, England and Downer's Grove, Illinois U.S.A. p502
[25] I. Breward, *New Dictionary of Theology* p550
[26] G. Parsons, (1988), *Religion in Victorian England Vol. 1 Traditions* Manchester University Press, Manchester and New York, In Association with The Open University. p84
[27] S.M. Houghton, (1980 reprinted 1991), *Sketches From Church History* Banner of Truth Trust, Edinburgh, Scotland. p182
[28] *Select Works of Jonathan Edwards Vol. 1.* Banner of Truth Trust, London, England, (1965) This volume also contains: *The Distinguishing Marks of the Work of the Spirit of God* and *An Account of the Revival in North Hampton 1740-42.*
[29] The details of these revivals are dealt with in fuller detail by Gerald Parsons in *Religion in Victorian Britain* Ch 6 "Emotion and Piety: Revivalism and Ritualism in Victorian Christianity." Manchester University Press, Manchester and New York. (1988)
[30] For a fuller treatment of these movements and their impact on Pentecostalism see D. William Faupel, (1996) *The Everlasting*

Gospel: The Significance of Eschatology in the Development of Pentecostal Thought Sheffield Academic Press, Sheffield, England pp54-76

[31] D. W. Bebbington, (1989) *Evangelicalism in Modern Britain: A History from the 1730s to the 1980s* Unwin Hyman Ltd. Reprinted Routledge, London and New York, (1993, 1995) pp151-180. See also Faupel *The Everlasting Gospel* p85-87.

[32] Bebbington, *Evangelicalism in Modern Britain* p173

[33] C.G. Finney, (last reprint 1973) *Power From On High* Victory Press, Eastbourne, Sussex.

[34] Bebbington, *Evangelicalism in Modern Britain* p164

[35] Gee, *The Pentecostal Movement* p4

[36] J. Gunstone, (1994) *Pentecost Comes to Church: Sacraments and Spiritual Gifts,* Darton, Longman and Todd, London. p23

[37] W.E. Boardman, (1860) *The Higher Christian Life* James Nisbet and Co. London,

[38] Parsons, *Religion in Victorian Britain* p222

[39] Bebbington, *Evangelicalism in Modern Britain* p174

[40] Gordon Lindsay has written a useful book on Dowie entitled: *The Life of John Alexander Dowie: A life of Trials, Tragedies and Triumph,* Voice of Healing Publishing Co. USA (1951) For more up-to-date and scholarly treatments of Dowie see Philip L. Cook, (1996) *Zion City, Illinois: Twentieth-Century Utopia,* Syracuse University Press. Also Grant Wacker, Chris R Armstrong, and Jay S. F. Blossom, "John Alexander Dowie: Harbinger of Pentecostal Power", in James R. Goff Jr. and Grant Wacker editors, *Portraits of a Generation: Early Pentecostal Leaders*, University of Kansas Press, Fayetteville, 2002,pp3-19.

[41] See Walter Hollenweger, (1972) *The Pentecostal Movement,* SCM Press, London, England. p354 See also Faupel pp116-135

[42] Allen, *The Unfailing Stream* p101

[43] Ian Randall, (1997) *Movements of Evangelical Spirituality in the Inter-war England,* PhD Thesis University of Wales, p290

[44] Peter Hocken adds an interesting section on the impact of Brethrenism upon the Charismatic Renewal in his Ph. D Dissertation, *Baptised in the Spirit: The Origins and Development of the Charismatic Movement in Great Britain,* University of Birmingham (1984) Appendix III p225ff. This was later printed in book form as: *Streams of Renewal: The Origins and Development of the Charismatic*

Movement in Great Britain, (1986) The Paternoster Press, Exeter, England,

[45] See *Church Doctrine and Practice,* published by The Precious Seed Committee (1970), a Brethren magazine, for a fuller explanation for many of these Brethren beliefs and practices.

[46] Randall, *Movements of Evangelical Spirituality in the inter-war England.* p291

[47] Douglas Petersen, (1996) *Not by Might nor by Power: A Pentecostal Theology of Social Concern in Latin America,* Regnum Books International in association with Paternoster Press, Carlisle, England p19,20

[48] Dispensationalists believe that all of human history is divided up into seven specific ages. It was the particular theological development of the Brethren theologian J.N. Darby. See Robert M. Anderson, (1979) *Vision of the Disinherited: The Making of American Pentecostalism*, Oxford University Press, Oxford and New York p39-41

[49] Cessationists believe that the gifts of the Spirit ceased with the Twelve Apostles.

[50] D. William Faupel, (1996) *The Everlasting Gospel: The Significance of Eschatology in the Development of Pentecostal Thought* Sheffield Academic Press, Sheffield, England.

[51] Edith Blumhofer stresses: "Darby's teaching played a significant role in shaping the context in which Pentecostalism emerged." *Restoring the Faith: The Assemblies of God, Pentecostalism and American Culture,* University of Ilinois Press, Urbana and Chicago (1993) p16.

[52] *The Millennial Kingdom,* Zondervan Publishing House, Michigan, USA.

[53] Philip Mauro, (reprinted 1974) *The Gospel of the Kingdom: An Examination of Dispensationalism* Reiner Publications, Swengel, PA. U.S,A p20

[54] Donald Gee refers to "the Rapture" in *The Pentecostal Movement* p2. Wynne Lewis wrote about it in the book *Pentecostal Doctrine.* (1976) Edited by P.S. Brewster, Elim Pentecostal Church, Cheltenham, England. pp259-271. Dispensationalism is also enshrined within the American Assemblies of God Statement of Fundamental Truths number 13 *The Blessed Hope* and 14 *The Millennial Reign of Jesus.* W. Hollenweger, *The Pentecostals,* pp 515,516.

[55] Anderson, *Vision of the Disinherited* and Douglas Petersen, *Not by*

Might nor by Power

[56] Bebbington also shows the impact of Brethrenism on the various holiness groups arising during the nineteenth century *Evangelicalism in Modern Britain* pp157-159

[57] Faupel, *The Everlasting Gospel* p19

[58] Bloch-Hoell, *The Pentecostal Movement* p173.

[59] Bloch-Hoell, *The Pentecostal Movement* p173.

[60] Faupel, *The Everlasting Gospel* p16

[61] Faupel, *The Everlasting Gospel* p17 and taken from D.W. Dayton (1987) *The Theological Roots of Pentecostalism*, Metuchen, NJ: The Scarecrow Press pp21-23

[62] Faupel, *The Everlasting Gospel* p17

[63] Faupel, *The Everlasting Gospel* p17

[64] D.W. Faupel, "Whither Pentecostalism?" *Pneuma: The Journal of the Society for Pentecostal Studies,* Vol. 15, No.1 Spring (1993) p21 Society for Pentecostal Studies, P.O. Box 2641 Gaithersburg, MD 20886, USA.

[65] Petersen, *Not by Might Nor By Power* p147

[66] Petersen, *Not by Might Nor By Power* p147

[67] Bloch-Hoell, *The Pentecostal Movement* p172

[68] N. Scotland *Charismatics and the Next Millennium: Do They Have A Future?* Hodder and Stoughton, London, Sydney and Auckland. (1995) p5.

[69] Ibid

Chapter 2: W. J. Seymour: Catalyst of Change

Traditionally, Pentecostal churches trace their roots to Azusa Street in Los Angeles. David A. Womack, however, traces the movement's roots to Charles Fox Parham in Topeka in Kansas on 1st January 1901.[70] These beginnings seem to centre on the incidence of speaking in tongues. However, tongues speaking or "glossolalia"[71] as it is sometimes called has been reported on numerous occasions.[72] David Allen suggests it was predated by seventy-six years under the influence of Alexander Scott, an associate minister of Edward Irving. Allen claims, Mary Campbell in West Scotland was apparently healed and baptised in the Spirit and spoke in tongues in spring of 1830.[73] So, what it so unique about Azusa Street? That is what this chapter seeks to explore.

The American Experience

It is Azusa Street under its leader W. J. Seymour (1870-1922), which is seen as the origin of the modern

Pentecostal movement. It happened, according to Donald Gee, on 9 April 1906.[74] Walter Hollenweger, however, says the first experience under Seymour happened in Bonnie Brae Street not Azusa Street. The argument concerning Pentecostal origins seems to turn on the occurrence of speaking in tongues. As there are various accounts of tongues before Azusa Street - Edward Irving and Charles Fox Parham to name two - it seems to me that we cannot base the argument for origins on incidents of glossolalia. Pentecostal origins must be based more firmly on the source and influence of its rapid growth. Not that speaking in tongues are unimportant but they are part of the process of the modern revival. For this we rightly, in my opinion, must look to Azusa Street and W. J. Seymour in particular. So how did it all come about?

W. J. Seymour was born in Centreville, Louisiana, the son of recently freed slaves.[75] No doubt his social position in America of the time gave him his social awareness. Harvey Cox calls him a "...social visionary...."[76] His desire for racial harmony and brotherhood was evidenced in the mixture of races in the early meetings. Frank Bartleman observed: "The color line has been washed away by the blood."[77] But Seymour was more than a social visionary. In fact it is doubtful if he would have liked such an appellation to himself. He saw himself, primarily, as a servant of God. So how did he arrive at this juncture in his life and what were the social and theological forces which made him the kind of man he was?

Little is known of Seymour between his birth and his arrival in Indianapolis in 1895 where he joined the Methodist Episcopal Church. Cecil M. Robeck fills in some of the blanks for us in his recent publication on Azusa Street entitled: *Azusa Street Mission and Revival: The Birth of The Global Pentecostal Movement.*[78] The Methodist Episcopal Church was a black congregation, according to Cox, in a mainly white denomination.[79] Seymour had moved to Cincinnati where he came under the influence of M.W. Knapp, the Methodist evangelist, who encouraged black people to attend his chapel and Bible School.[80] It was here, Faupel says, he was "...exposed to the doctrines of the Pre-millennial return of Christ, and healing in the atonement." as well as querying denominationalism and sectarianism.[81] In Cincinnati Seymour also encountered another group, "The Evening Light Saints."[82] They espoused the belief of a great outpouring of the Spirit before the return of Christ. Cox adds that this group taught the concept that God was calling together a "...purified and racially inclusive church...."[83]

It was on his move to Houston in Texas, however, that Seymour's spiritual ministry began to crystallise and take shape. Lucy Farrow, whom he had succeeded as pastor of the Holiness Church in Houston, returned from Kansas where she had been working for Charles Fox Parham. She related to him the experience of speaking in tongues which she had encountered under Parham. Seymour felt instinctively that it was of God. To Seymour this was the sign of the Coming of Christ which he so longed for. When Parham moved his Bible School to Houston, Seymour enrolled. He was so hungry for this teaching he was even willing to sit in the hall to listen to the lectures so as not to offend the racial sensitivities of the white Texan population.[84] It is thought this segregation was enforced by Parham himself as he appeared to have sympathies with the racist tendencies of the southern states. Cox says he was "A Ku Klux Klan sympathiser...."[85] Hollenweger too says Parham also believed in "...the British Israel theory"[86] which tends to elevate the superiority of the Anglo-Saxon races. It was Hollenweger and his student D.J. Nelson who seem to be the first to brand Parham as a racist.

In recent years, however, this socio-racist perspective on Parham and Pentecostal origins has been challenged with great tenacity. The issue was brought to the fore during seminars on Charles Fox Parham at the World Pentecostal Conference in Los Angeles in 2001. This was in many ways the result of others questioning the Hollenweger/Nelson perspective on the socio-racist issue of Pentecostal origins. J.R. Goff had already queried Parham's alleged racism in his book: *Fields White unto Harvest: Charles F. Parham and the Missionary Origins of Pentecostalism*.[87] It had been thought that Parham's reaction to the revival at Azusa Street was blatant racism. William Faupel takes up Goff's point claiming that Goff argued that it was "... a little more complex."[88] Faupel asserts that Goff believed Parham had a paternalistic attitude to 'blacks' which was 'more enlightened' than most of his southern counterparts. The argument seems to turn on Hollenweger's academic bias concerning Parham's racism and this was taken up by Nelson, Hollenweger's student, in his PhD thesis. Perhaps this perspective had more to do with the apartheid problems in South Africa at the time of the initial studies with Hollenweger and Nelson, then super-imposing the racial dimension on to Pentecostal origins and Parham in particular.

In the light of this one has to ask who allowed Seymour to benefit from the teaching at his Bible College and who it was who paid for him to go to Los Angeles in the first place. It may be surprising to learn that it was Parham; hardly the act of a racist. True, he had to be careful not to offend the sensitivities of southern whites by steering a middle course through it all but this has to be seen in the context of the time and culture. The issue of Parham's racism is an on-going debate within Pentecostal academic circles and is set to continue for the foreseeable future.

It was while Seymour was in Houston he came into contact with Neelly Terry from the Santa Fe Ave. Holiness Church. She was so impressed with Seymour she invited him to come to Los Angeles with a view to pastoring the congregation. He responded positively and arrived in Los Angeles on 22nd February 1906. At first he was well received and continued his ministry acceptably until 4th March but it was on their discovery of his views on glossolalia as the 'initial evidence' of the baptism in the Spirit that the split occurred. On his arrival to conduct the evening service Sunday 4th March he found that the leader, Mrs Hutchins, had "locked the door and refused to admit him."[89]

After Seymour had been locked out of the Sante Fe Ave Holiness Church[90] for preaching on the necessity of tongues as a sign of the baptism in the Spirit others left with him. It seems he moved around holding meetings in various homes. It was in one of these, the home of Richard Asberry [91] in Bonnie Brae Street, that the group first experienced the baptism in the Holy Spirit. It was this experience which convinced Seymour of the truth of all he believed and it motivated him to promote it at all costs.

Catalysts of the Spirit

The revival began through prayer meetings held in the home of Edward and Mattie Lee. Initially Seymour and the Lees spent time in prayer together. Gradually they were joined by people mainly from East Ninth and Santa Fe Avenue Holiness churches as well as Frank Bartleman. The group became so large they had to move to a more spacious place. The home of Richard and Ruth Asberry on Bonnie Brae Street was chosen. This situation pertained for some weeks with regular prayer times. The breakthrough came when Seymour laid hands on Edward Lee for healing and it was suggested they pray for him to be baptised in the Spirit. As they did so he fell on to the floor and spoke with tongues. Later they went to the meeting in the home of the Asberrys where Seymour shared what had happened to Lee. As he was finishing his narration of the thrilling event someone in the group also began to speak in tongues. From this time onwards word began to spread of the new revival which had just begun. Up to this point the whole thing was rather similar to happenings in Topeka, Kansas when Agnes Ozman spoke in tongues under Charles Fox Parham's ministry so why was Azusa Street so different? The difference was in the way Seymour set about propagating the new revival.

The first thing he did was to look for an appropriate place to meet on a regular basis. He found this at 312 Azusa

Street, Los Angeles. This building had been a church turned into a stable. The problem was it has been the target of an arson attack and the building was in a deplorable state. It was dirty and smelly and unusable. Robeck gives a fuller account of this in his book so we will not delay over the details here.[92] The people sat on planks over nail kegs and others brought various forms of seating. The pulpit was a crate used for shipping shoes to dealers over which was draped a simple piece of cotton cloth. The next thing he did was to organise the leadership of the church with a working staff along with formulating a doctrinal basis for the embryonic movement. Worship, preaching and teaching and printing were also important aspects of it all. Seymour was more than a simple 'black' preacher; he was a leader and an organiser and his skills in these areas helped to project the emerging revival onto the public stage. His ability to steer the whole thing honourably and righteously was a crucial lynchpin in propelling the new movement forward.

It was in this humble environment that God moved mightily to begin to bring about a movement which would eventually straddle the globe. People came from all over America and beyond to witness and experience what they believed was the latter day revival before the coming of Christ. How strange that the ministry of

Catalysts of the Spirit

such a man, with no formal theological education and a black man at that should have made the impact he has on twentieth century Christianity. Yet he did just that. Seymour's ministry impacted the lives of various people who went on to establish Pentecostal churches and gatherings not only in America but throughout the world. Many of these churches and denominations are still in the forefront of Pentecostal activity today. In this Seymour saw the promised revival to restore the church and break down all the social and racial barriers along with it. D.J. Nelson highlights this in his doctoral thesis on Seymour saying: "Seymour's far-sighted leadership harnessed the power released in glossolalic worship, to break down the color line barrier - along with serious divisions of humanity and create a new dimension of Christian community."[93] Perhaps this is one reason why Seymour promoted and marketed the Pentecostal experience; the power of its social implications. In so doing Seymour made Azusa Street the true origin of Pentecostalism as a modern phenomenon not the crisis experience itself nor the manifestation of tongues.

Yet it is only in recent years that Seymour's role in the formation of modern Pentecostalism has begun to be acknowledged. Seymour, a black uneducated preacher, was the undoubted mainstay and "catalyst"[94] of it all.

Harvey Cox asserts also that without him there can be no real understanding of Pentecostal origins.[95] So what were the effects of the revival and its influence on American and global Christianity?

Branches over the Wall

Seymour's influence was chiefly through the medium of writing.[96] He published his own magazine, *Apostolic Faith,* which was sent out free to anyone who wanted it. Reports in the newspapers also projected Seymour and Azusa Street into the religious limelight of the day. Much of it was not very complimentary.[97] This helped, however, to bring people from all over America and the world to see for themselves. It also fuelled desires for a similar move of God in every country. Those whom Seymour and Azusa Street influenced were numerous and other fellowships and individuals were greatly affected. Due to contact with Seymour and his ministry they and their churches changed to become Pentecostal in experience and practice whilst others started new Pentecostal works.

C.H. Mason and the Church of God in Christ. Although Mason's fellowship had already been established since 1897 it became a Pentecostal Church after his meeting with Seymour. Mason, another black preacher like Seymour himself, was baptised in the Spirit in Azusa Street in 1906. On reporting his experience to the church a split occurred.[98] Mason reformed the split church as a Pentecostal fellowship. This had a great effect on the prestige of Pentecostalism in America as Mason had the right to ordain ministers.

G.B. Cashwell and the Pentecostal Holiness Church.
Cashwell also received the baptism in the Holy Spirit at Azusa Street in 1906. On his return he influenced his own church, the Holiness Church of North Carolina (HCNC), to adopt Pentecostal teaching. Through his influence two other Holiness churches merged with HCNC - The Fire-Baptised Holiness Church and The Tabernacle Pentecostal Church - to form the Pentecostal Holiness Church. This was changed in 1975 to The International Pentecostal Holiness Church.

A. J. Tomlinson and the Church of God (Cleveland).
It was during Cashwell's preaching at a Church of God (Cleveland) general assembly in 1908 that A.J. Tomlinson claims to have spoken in tongues. This not only changed Tomlinson's life, it changed the very theological character of the Church of God. Up to this point the Church of God was regarded as a holiness church even though they had previously experienced speaking in tongues during

a revival.[99] David Allen actually says the Church of God was "...historically speaking, the first Pentecostal denomination...."[100] However, it needs to be said that Allen seems to base this assertion on the experience of speaking in tongues. This is not a good basis for such a claim as others, such as the Catholic Apostolic Church under Edward Irving experienced glossolalia prior to Seymour. They could equally claim they were the first Pentecostals. Other factors need to be considered such as structuring along Pentecostal lines with a distinctly Pentecostal identity and statement of faith. In this sense either the Church of God in Christ or the Pentecostal Holiness Church could be seen as the first Pentecostal denomination. They reformed themselves along Pentecostal lines after their leaders had been to Azusa Street. However the Church of God (Cleveland) was restructured by Tomlinson after his Spirit baptism under Cashwell in 1908.[101] Tomlinson later split from The Church of God (Cleveland) to form the Church of God of Prophecy about 1920. Hollenweger gives a chart showing the various deviations from the original Church of God in his book *The Pentecostals.*[102]

Unfortunately, time and space do not permit the inclusion of all those ministers and movements which were influenced by Seymour but the foregoing are among the leaders of early Pentecostalism. [103] Harvey Cox's assessment of Seymour would seem to be justified in that without him we would not have a full understanding of the Pentecostal movement. In the light of all that has been said it would seem justifiable to view Azusa Street as the source and origin of modern day Pentecostalism.

The Parting of the Ways

Seymour was a typical Holiness preacher. He accepted the two stage process of grace in the life of the Christian - conversion and sanctification. However, in line with his mentor, C. F. Parham, he added a third stage - that of the baptism of the Holy Spirit;[104] though not everyone agreed however.

W. H. Durham.[105] (1873-1912) One of the most influential leaders affected by Seymour was W.H. Durham, Baptist pastor of Chicago's North Avenue Mission.[106] He received the baptism in the Spirit in Azusa Street under Seymour in 1907. After that he devoted himself to the Pentecostal ministry. Durham, however, fell out of favour with Seymour when he began to teach an experience of power based on his teaching of "the finished work of Christ."[107] In this he was taking issue with the current Pentecostal-Holiness teaching of Parham and Seymour.

Durham interpreted sanctification as an ongoing experience of the work of the Spirit in the life of the believer.[108] He was eventually "expelled from the Apostolic Faith Church"[109] by Seymour for his teaching. Valdez likens Seymour's action towards Durham as that of Saul and David and "Like Saul he began making mistakes. The most grave was chaining and padlocking the Azusa Street Mission door shut."[110] Durham's teaching signalled the beginnings of disunity which together with the New Issue concerning the Trinity split the Pentecostal movement in three ways.[111] Hollenweger says of Durham that: "... he has remained up to the present day the one original Pentecostal theologian of the American Pentecostal movement." [112]

Under Durham's ministry many influential leaders were raised up to form other Pentecostal fellowships both in America and abroad. [113]Aimee Semple McPherson came into her ministry as a result of Durham's influence. She went on to found the flourishing International Church of the Foursquare Gospel. Not only did she claim to have been healed of a broken ankle through Durham's ministry but she met and married her first husband, Robert Semple, through his work. It was McPherson who gave Pentecostalism its profoundest theological definition - Jesus Christ as Saviour, Baptiser in the Holy Spirit, Healer and Coming King.

American Assemblies of God. Others whom Durham influenced were E.N. Bell and Howard Goss, two founders of Assemblies of God, which grew to become the largest Pentecostal denomination in the world. R.M. Anderson observes: "...few could have been in doubt as to where they stood on the issue of sanctification."[114] Indeed the keynote address by M. M. Pinson at the Assemblies of God Convention in Hot Springs, Arkansas in 1914 was "The Finished Work of Christ". According to Cox: "...Durham's disciples joined others to organize a rival denomination, the Assemblies of God..." [115] This may be a debatable point but it at least shows the extent of Durham's teaching on the fledgling movement.

The far-reaching effects of Seymour's ministry and that of Azusa Street are readily seen in the influence brought to bear in the lives of others who in turn affected their own fellowship or in founding new Pentecostal denominations.

Roots of Prosperity Teaching

It has been argued that right at the outset of the Pentecostal revival heterodoxy was growing alongside its traditional orthodoxy. It was a falsehood, it is thought, which incorporated the latest philosophical ideas which were rising at the time. These new ideas were coming out of Emerson College of Oratory, Boston and espoused by Essek William Kenyon (1867-1948).[116]

Kenyon was a student of Emerson College[117] which, it is said, taught the New Thought philosophy of P.P. Quimby with its emphasis on health and healing, prosperity and happiness through the exercise of the mind.[118] Kenyon referred to it as the positive confession of the Word of God: "What I confess, I possess."[119] In essence it seems to have had much in common with Mary Baker Eddy's Christian Science beliefs. Her idea of 'mind over matter' was developed through contact with Quimby who supposedly healed her through the power of auto-suggestion.[120] Norman Vincent Peale's positive thinking may also be traced to this source.

Basically, 'Positive Confession', as it came to be termed, believes in the power of the spoken word based on the Word of God. When we claim things by faith we speak them into existence. L. Lovett states: "From Quimby, William Branham, E.W. Kenyon and John G. Lake, a view of God emerged that is currently espoused by Hagin, Copeland, Capps and Price."[121] It is firmly believed by many thinkers that Quimby and Emerson College were extremely influential on ministers of the new emerging Pentecostal movement. Many of them saw in this teaching a foundation for Pentecostal theology. Since that time it has grown and taken root in Pentecostal theology and thinking. It has now become so interlinked it is hard to disentangle it from its more orthodox roots. So who did it affect?

J. G. Lake (1870-1935) Lake worked with Seymour closely in Azusa Street, along with Tom Hezmalhalch. Eventually he and Hezmalhalch went out as missionaries to South Africa. They established the Apostolic Faith Mission of South Africa in 1908. Lake had been associated with Alexander Dowie and his Zion City for some time and it was through Dowie his wife was healed of tuberculosis. Thomas Hezmalhalch, an Englishman, had immigrated to America in the 1880s. From there he went to South Africa with Lake and became the first president of the AFM in South Africa.[122] Although there is no real evidence of Hezmalhalch espousing this new teaching, Lake became a firm advocate.

F.F. Bosworth (1877-1958) The same can be said of F.F. Bosworth who worked for a time with Seymour.[123] Bosworth was influenced by both John Alexander Dowie and E.W. Kenyon.[124] He was at first a member of the newly formed Assemblies of God but left over the issue of tongues as the initial evidence. Through the teaching of men like Lake and Bosworth New Thought philosophy was thought to have been gradually introduced into Pentecostalism. This has come to be expressed in various faith-formula theologies - Positive Confession, Word of Faith and "Name and Claim it". From this teaching other groups emerged such as the Latter Rain Movement[125] and the work of healing evangelists like William Branham and T.L. Osborne. Osborne, in fact, refers to both Bosworth and Lake in his book: *Healing the Sick* and even gives an extract from Kenyon's book *Jesus the Healer.*[126] R.M. Riss confirms this: "Various aspects of his theology became an important influence on such diverse people as W. J. "Ern" Baxter, F.F. Bosworth, David Nunn, T.L. Osborne, Jimmy Swaggart and many others."[127] The more recent evangelists such as Kenneth Hagin, Kenneth Copeland and others are also the legitimate heirs of Kenyon's Positive Confession and Word of Faith Teaching.[128] They both quote him extensively in their writings. Oral Roberts too may be associated with this school due to his emphasis on prosperity teaching, but he is generally regarded as a classical Pentecostal. Benny Hinn may also be associated with Kenyon's ideas. [129]

This unorthodox strain in Pentecostalism has begun to cause increasing concern due to some of the unwise statements its exponents are making. Hunt and McMahon give quotations[130] from various writers of the extremes this teaching is going to. John G. Lake claimed that man "...is part of God himself...God intends us to be gods." Earl Paulk claims that, "Just as dogs have puppies and cats have kittens, so God has little gods." Kenneth Copeland is also reported as saying: "...Well now you don't have a God in you. You are one."[131] Such 'godism' is a worrying trend for many Pentecostals.[132] To them it is so much akin to New Thought philosophy it is almost startling. The 1916 statement of the International New Thought Alliance shows the Divinity of man and his Infinite Possibilities through the creative powers of constructive thinking. It goes on to say that by obeying the voice of the indwelling Presence we can have Power, Health and Prosperity.[133] Man's divine nature is a crucial element to Quimby's metaphysics.

However, the association of Kenyon's teaching with New Thought has been heavily criticised in a two other studies: *E.W. Kenyon and His Message of Faith: The True Story*[134] and *Quenching the Spirit: Discover the Real Spirit Behind the Charismatic Controversy.*[135] McIntyre claims that Kenyon could not have been exposed to New Thought philosophy, if any, as it was in its infancy in Emerson College when Kenyon was there. Kenyon did attend here during the academic year 1892-93 but New Thought's chief exponent in the college, Ralph Waldo Trine, was only beginning to study it at that time. DeArteaga, however, accepts the fact that Kenyon may have taken some New Thought ideas on board but contends he rejected its Metaphysical and Gnostic core and seriously criticised the known exponents of the philosophy such as Christian Science and the Unity Movement. Indeed both these writers point out that many early Pentecostal leaders could have read and been aware of much New Thought literature and may even have endorsed aspects of it without espousing it as a system of belief. This is because Emerson College had strong associations with evangelical Christianity and any New Thought concept would be filtered through its evangelical basis. The Evangelical Alliance have sought recently to give some guidance to its member churches with the publication of *Faith, Health and Prosperity*136 but this seems to rely heavily on the work of Dan McConnell and others against Word Faith and prosperity groups so in this sense it does not add anything further to the debate.

The New Issue. Early in its history a theological controversy erupted which threatened to split the emerging Pentecostal movement down the middle. It came to be known as the New Issue. It was a theological debate centring on the formula for baptism. Some felt it should be administered in the name of Jesus only whilst other argued for the Trinitarian formula of Father, Son and Holy Spirit. The emphasis on the name of Jesus caused a number of Pentecostal leaders to question the orthodox view of the Trinity. In time this led to the establishing of "Oneness" churches which taught there was no Trinity and that Jesus was Father, Son and Holy Spirit. Some Oneness teachers seemed to teach an old heresy called Modalistic Monarchianism, in that they said Jesus revealed himself in three forms in three different eras – in the Old Testament as the Father, in the Gospels as the Son and now in the church age as the Holy Spirit. Others saw it more as a representative name. However, as it did not involve Seymour or Azusa Street we will not delay over this.[137]

W.J. Seymour was indeed a catalyst for change as this chapter, I trust, clearly shows. Through his ministry in Azusa Street he influenced, directly and indirectly, many of Pentecostalism's early pioneers. He also influenced the formation of every major Pentecostal denomination in America and throughout the world. Recent studies are endeavouring to correct the injustice done to him by now giving him the recognition which he rightly deserves. W.J. Seymour left the Christian world and the Pentecostal Church in particular, a rich fourfold legacy.

Firstly Seymour gives a historical link with both Holiness and non-Holiness traditions in the Christian Church. The origins of Pentecostalism within the Wesleyan tradition and its changes under Keswick influence as well as the controversies over Durham are a constant reminder of the need for tolerance among Christians.

Secondly there is the theological legacy. Although largely uneducated in formal theological training he showed a remarkable astuteness in theological matters. H.V. Synan says of Seymour: "Probably the only theological training he ever received was in Parham's Houston School."[138] One of his greatest contributions was to put glossolalia into a broader theological and social context, "...unifying the whole church across the boundaries of language, race and nationality."[139] D.J. Nelson puts it succinctly: "Parham thought glossalalia was proof of an experience whilst Seymour saw it as the means to a restored community... a truly inclusive church."[140] Seymour and Azusa Street became the catalyst of spiritual change by bringing together all the strands of holiness and evangelical teaching and applying them in practical terms to the benefit of the whole Christian church.

Another very important aspect to Seymour's ministry was the social element, which is only just beginning to

Catalysts of the Spirit

be realised. The great desire of his heart was to see the social and racial walls, so acute in America at the time, brought down. He saw the Pentecostal experience of the baptism in the Holy Spirit as a means to that end. A more recent study by Cecil Robeck says much the same thing in that Seymour and Azusa Street reached out to "...the marginalized – the poor, women, and people of color."[141] G.B. Cashwell the "European-American Holiness evangelist...." was confronted with racism through his experience of the baptism in the Holy Spirit says Dale T. Irvin. He continues: "Only after dying to his racism could he seek the laying on of hands from Seymour and other African-Americans, leading to his Pentecostal baptism in 1906."[142] D.J. Nelson deals with this question of racism at great length in his doctoral thesis on Seymour showing Seymour's social pioneering spirit.[143] Cox remarks too that the Assemblies of God was formed by disciples of Durham so that "...white ministers would not have to be led by blacks."[144] Cox though may be relying too heavily here on Hollenweger and Nelson.

All things considered the socio-racial aspect of Pentecostal origins still has much to commend it if we are careful not to stretch it beyond credibility. There seems no doubt in my mind that Pentecostalism offered Afro-American people a glimmer of hope in an otherwise oppressive environment. It was all bound up in the levelling nature of spiritual gifts and their propensity to unify the body of Christ as well as their potential to signal the soon coming of Christ to bring to an end all injustices.

Without really knowing it, perhaps, Seymour was also pre-empting the feminist revolution by fifty years by including women in crucial areas of ministry and church government and allowing freedom of expression through the gifts of the Spirit. As Seymour says himself: "It is contrary to scripture that woman should not have her part in the salvation work to which God has called her...."[145] Although this is fairly advanced for its time, even by Holiness standards which permitted more freedom than most for women, he did not go all the way. He still restricted the acts of ordination and baptism to men.[146]

Lastly and, perhaps, more controversially there was an ecumenical dimension to Seymour's work. It was not akin to the modern concept of ecumenism as we understand it today however. Faupel intimates Seymour viewed denominations and creeds as man-made. This antipathy came, possibly, from his association with Knapp and The Evening Light Saints who both called them into question.[147] Yet, unlike them he acknowledged: "All these denominations are our brethren."[148] Faupel adds that

Catalysts of the Spirit

Seymour challenged critics of denominational churches and encouraged those baptised in the Spirit within them to remain as "leaven".[149] He also welcomed visitors from all the Christian traditions. His vision of an all inclusive church embraced more than race and colour. It included all branches of the Church as well. Frank Bartleman, who attended Azusa Street in the early days of the revival, caught something of the ecumenical spirit of the place saying: "When will God's people become 'one flock' with 'one shepherd', Jesus, as he promised? It is surely time to pray as Jesus prayed 'that they may be one that the world may believe'."[150]

The question needs to be asked, concerning these early Pentecostals at the beginning of the twentieth century, did they see ecumenism and unity in the same way as we do at the beginning of the twenty-first century. It may be a moot point but it is more likely that they believed the church would become Pentecostal and embrace the whole of Pentecostal theology and practice. Cecil Robeck, an advocate of Ecumenism, admits that Pentecostals rejected ecumenism at first.[151] Harvey Cox agrees saying: "The early Pentecostals were obviously not ecumenists, at least not in today's sense."[152] What these early Pentecostals understood by unity, it seems to me, was based on a

Pentecostal/Evangelical understanding of returning to New Testament principles in beliefs and practices.

Conclusion

As we can see, W. J. Seymour was uniquely vital to the birth of the Pentecostal movement; a catalyst indeed, igniting the fire of revival which would soon encompass the world in the twentieth century and beyond it. Although Seymour's influence on the Pentecostal movement did not last very long, it was not through lack of leadership. D. J. Nelson asserts it was precisely the opposite in that "...he was all too effective and successful as a leader."[153] Nelson suggests it was his colour which was against him. He quotes W.E.B. DuBois as saying: "The problem of the twentieth century is the problem of the color line."[154] This though seems too over-simplistic an explanation. However, to suggest Seymour's loss of influence in the American Pentecostal church at large was due to racism is to do an injustice to the vast array of genuine Christians in that country both black and white. The answer must lie in the multifarious nature of the movement drawing on all shades of theological opinion and practice.

God had begun something in this enigmatic and apparently insignificant Afro-American to challenge the

Catalysts of the Spirit

world concerning salvation, equality and brotherhood. The Pentecostal flame soon spread to various parts of America and Canada attracting many seeking the power of the Holy Spirit. Visitors came from all over the world, some hungry and seeking God; some, no doubt, curious and seeking sensationalism with others seeking a means to criticise the emerging movement; yet, in W.J. Seymour, the Pentecostal ministry had begun in earnest.

---

[70]David A. Womack, Complier & Editor (1993) *Pentecostal Experience: The Writings of Donald Gee* Gospel Publishing House, Springfield, Missouri. p11

[71]A fuller account of this and the differing terminologies, is given by R. P. Spittler in *Dictionary of Pentecostal and Charismatic Movements* pp335-334

[72]C. Brumback, (1947) *What Meaneth This?* Gospel Publishing House, Springfield Missouri, USA. Ch 6 outlines incidents of speaking in tongues and other gifts of the Spirit in church history.

[73]David Allen, (1994) *The Unfailing Stream* Sovereign World, Tonbridge, England p86

[74]Gee, *The Pentecostal Movement* p12

[75]Faupel, *The Everlasting Gospel* p195

[76]Cox, *Fire from Heaven* p48

[77]Frank Bartleman, (reprint 1985) *How Pentecost Came to Los Angeles* (Los Angeles: F. Bartleman) Garland Publishing, Inc., p54

[78]Cecil M. Robeck Jr, (2006) *Azusa Street Mission and Revival:*

Harry Letson

The Birth of the Global Pentecostal Movement, Thomas Nelson, Nashville, Tennessee. USA p17ff

[79] Cox, *Fire from Heaven* p48

[80] Faupel, *The Everlasting Gospel* p195

[81] Faupel, *The Everlasting Gospel* p197

[82] The official title of this group, Church of God, Reformation, is given by H.V. Synan: *Dictionary of Pentecostal and Charismatic Movements* p780 Blumhofer explains why this group calls itself by this name in *Restoring the Faith* p29

[83] Cox, *Fire from Heaven* p49

[84] Cox, *Fire from Heaven* p49

[85] Cox, *Fire from Heaven* p49

[86] Hollenweger, *The Pentecostals* p22 See also Cecil M. Robeck, (2006) *Azusa Streetreet Mission and Revival: The Birth of the Global Pentecostal Movement.* Thomas Nelson, Nashville. Tn. USA p40

[87] J.R. Goff, (1988) *Fields White unto Harvest: Charles F. Parham and the Missionary Origins of Pentecostalism.* Fayetteville, AR: University of Arkansas.

[88] Faupel, p209

[89] Robeck, *Azusa Streetreet Mission and Revival* p63

[90] A.C. Valdez Sr. says it was a Nazarene Church. *Fire on Azusa Street: An Eye-Witness Account* Gift Publication, Costa Mesa, California, USA. (1980) p18

[91] Petersen says the surname is Sperrys, *Not By Might Nor By Power* p13. Anderson in *Vision of the Disinherited* has it Asbury p65

[92] Robeck, *Azusa Street Mission and Revival* p69ff

[93] D. J. Nelson, (1981) *For Such A Time As This: The Story of Bishop W.J. Seymour* PhD Thesis, University of Birmingham, England. p9

[94] H.V. Synan. "...in recent years Seymour's place as the catalyst of the worldwide Pentecostal movement has been assured." "William Joseph Seymour" *Dictionary of Pentecostal and Charismatic Movements* p781

[95] Harvey Cox, (1996) *Fire from Heaven* Cassell, Londonp48

[96] Malcolm J. Taylor (1994) *Publish and Be Blessed: A Case Study of Early Pentecostal Publishing History* PhD Thesis University of

Birmingham

[97] Cox, p59 and Hollenweger p23 both mention accounts from the press of the happenings in Azusa Street.

[98] Blumhofer, *Restoring the Faith*

[99] Cox, *Fire from Heaven* p73

[99] Both Hollenweger *The Pentecostals* p48 and Allen *The Unfailing Stream* p102-103

[100] Allen, *The Unfailing Stream* p103

[101] Cox, *Fire from Heaven* p73

[102] Hollenweger, *The Pentecostals* p49

[103] Carl Brumback deals with many of these early ministers and particularly the founding fathers of AoG in *Suddenly from Heaven: A History of Assemblies of God* Gospel Publishing House, Springfield, Missouri (1961)

[104] Hollenweger gives more information in his book *The Pentecostals* p25. See also Edith Bloomhoffer's, "William H. Durham: Years of Creativity, Years of Dissent." In *Portraits of a Generation*, Ed. James R.Goff Jr. and Grant Wacker, University of Arkansas Press, 2002, pp.123-142.

[105] See Edith Bloomhoffer's, "William H. Durham: Years of Creativity, Years of Dissent." In *Portraits of a Generation*, Ed. James R.Goff Jr. and Grant Wacker, University of Arkansas Press, 2002, pp123-142

[106] Faupel, *The Everlasting Gospel* p232

[107] See Faupel, *The Everlasting Gospel* pp237-240 for a brief definition of this.

[108] Faupel, *The Everlasting Gospel* pp238-239

[109] Hollenweger, *The Pentecostals* p24

[110] Valdez, *Fire on Azusa Street* p26

[111] Faupel, *The Everlasting Gospel* p229

[112] Hollenweger, *The Pentecostals* p25

[113] Faupel, *The Everlasting Gospel* pp238-239

[114] R.M. Anderson, *Vision of the Disinherited* p166-168 See Faupel *The Everlasting Gospel* Ch 7

[115] Cox, *Fire from Heaven* p62

[116] See D.R. McConnell, *The Promise of Health and Wealth: A Historical and Biblical Analysis of the Modern Faith Movements*, Hodder and Stoughton, London and other locations (1990) p29ff for a detailed outline of Kenyon and his life and work. See also T. Smail,

A. Walker and N. Wright of the C.S. Lewis Centre, Kings College, University of London, in their article: "'Revelation Knowledge' and Knowledge of Revelation: The Faith Movement and the Question of Heresy." *Journal of Pentecostal Theology*, Issue 5 (1994) pp57-77

[117] McConnell, *The Promise of Health and Wealth* p137

[118] See Russell Chandler's comparison of New Thought and New Age in his book *Understanding New Age*, Word Publishing, Milton Keynes, England (1989) also various other publishers and locations. p205,206

[119] Attributed to Kenyon by McConnell, *The Promise of Health and Wealth* p140

[120] Walter Martin, (1965 Last edition 1992) *The Kingdom of the Cults*, Bethany House Publishers, Minneapolis, Minnesota, USA p127, 128.

[121] L. Lovett, *Dictionary of Pentecostal and Charismatic Movements* p719

[122] Hollenweger, *The Pentecostals* p120

[123] See photograph in *Dictionary of Pentecostal and Charismatic Movements* p33

[124] B. Barron, (undated) *The Health and Wealth Gospel*, InterVarsity Press, Downers Grove USA. p45&61&69

[125] D. Hunt & T.A. McMahon, (1985) *The Seduction of Christianity: Spiritual Discernment for the Last Days*, Harvest Publishers, Eugene, Oregon. USA. p219. See also R.M. Riss, (1987) *The Latter Rain Movement and the Mid-Century Evangelical Awakening*, Ontario, Canada.

[126] T.L. Osborne, (1959) *Healing the Sick* T.L. Osborne Evangelistic Association U.S.A etc. p105

[127] Riss, *Dictionary of Pentecostal and Charismatic Movements* p517

[128] McConnell, *The Promise of Health and Wealth* p50 & Barron *The Health and Wealth Gospel* p331ff

[129] G.R. Fisher, M. Goedelman & others, (1995, 3rd edition 1996) *The Confusing World of Benny Hinn*, Personal Freedom Outreach Publication, Bicester, England and other locations. p2

[130] Quoted in Hunt and McMahon, *The Seduction of Christianity* p219

[131] Hunt & McMahon, *The Seduction of Christianity* p84 see also on the same page Price and Capps.

[132] Hank Hanegraaff, (1994) *Christianity in Crisis*, Word Books,

Catalysts of the Spirit

Word Publishing, Milton Keynes and other locations. (1993) p331ff. For a thought provoking and balanced view see the article by Smail, Walker and Wright, *the Journal of Pentecostal Theology*, Issue 5 pp57-77

[133] *Encyclopaedia Britannica*, "New Thought" London and other locations, 15th Edition (1992) Vol. 8 p644

[134] Joe MacIntyre, (1997) *E.W. Kenyon and His Message of Faith: The True Story.* Creation House, Strang Communication Co. Florida USA

[135] William DeArteaga, (1992) *Quenching the Spirit: Discover the Real Spirit Behind the Charismatic Movement* Creation House, Strang Communication Co. Florida USA

[136] Andrew Perriman, (2003) *Faith, Health & Wealth*, Paternoster Press, Carlisle UK & Waynesboro, GA.

[137] The New Issue is referred to briefly by Donald Gee *The Pentecostal Movement* p124 though Carl Brumback deals extensively with the issues of Oneness Pentecostalism in his book *God in Three Persons* Pathway Press, Cleveland, Tennessee, U.S.A. (1959). For a more up-to-date treatment see G. A Boyd's book: *Oneness Pentecostals and the Trinity* Baker Book House, Grand Rapids, Michigan, USA.(1992) A condensed version of it all is given by D.A. Reed in the *Dictionary of Pentecostal and Charismatic Movements* pp640-651

[138] H.V. Synan, (1971 3rd reprint 1977) *The Holiness-Pentecostal Movement in the United States.* William B. Erdmans Publishing Co. Grand Rapids, Mich. USA. p105

[139] Dale T. Irvin, "Drawing All Together In one Bond of Love: The Ecumenical Vision of William J. Seymour and The Azusa Streetreet Revival." *Journal of Pentecostal Theology* Issue 6 (1995) p40

[140] Nelson, *For Such A Time As This* p11

[141] Robeck, (2006) *The Azusa Streetreet Mission and Revival: The Birth of Global Pentecostal Movement* p13

[142] Dale T. Irvin, *Journal of Pentecostal Theology* Issue 6 (1995) p46

[143] Nelson, *For Such A Time As This: The Story of W.J. Seymour* Ph.D. Thesis University of Birmingham, England (1981).

[144] Cox, *Fire from Heaven* p62

[145] *The Apostolic Faith* September 1907 p3 Quoted by Irvin in J.P.T 6 (1995) p47

[146] Seymour, *Doctrines and Discipline* 1915 p92 Quoted by Irvin in J.P.T 6 (1995) p47

[147] Faupel, *The Everlasting Gospel* p197
[148] *The Apostolic Faith* September 1907 p2 Quoted by Irvin in the *Journal of Pentecostal Theology* (1995) p44
[149] Faupel, *The Everlasting Gospel* p198
[150] Frank Bartleman, (1980) *Azusa Street: The Roots of Modern-Day Pentecost* Logos International, Plainfield, N.J. p158
[151] Cecil Robeck Jr, "Taking Stock of Pentecostalism: The Personal Reflections of a Retiring Editor" *Pneuma: The Journal of the Society for Pentecostal Studies* Vol. 15, No 1, Spring 1993 p39
[152] Cox, *Fire from Heaven* p74
[153] Nelson, *For Such A Time As This* p12
[154] Nelson, *For Such A Time As This* p15 DuBois *The Souls of Black Folk* Signet Classics, New York (1969 originally printed 1903)

Chapter 3: T.B. Barratt: Catalyst of Progress

A few months after the Azusa Street outpouring, a Methodist minister from Norway was on a fund-raising trip in America. Anderson notes that he was not only singularly unsuccessful in this but that he had experienced a number of personal tragedies which had left him quite dejected.[155] On reading a report in Seymour's journal: *Apostolic Faith* (September 1906)[156] concerning the revival in Los Angeles he was deeply stirred.[157] He wrote off to Seymour[158] and the replies convinced him that this was what he needed. Unable to afford the journey to Los Angeles he sought God for himself and was baptised in the Spirit and spoke in tongues, Gee says, in New York in October 1906.[159] The man was T.B. Barratt, the son of an English immigrant to Norway. Gee notes that some people reported seeing a light above Barratt's head like cloven tongues of fire. However, Barratt says he was alone on the occasion of his Spirit-baptism and did not speak in tongues "...until five weeks later at a prayer meeting with some friends."[160] Perhaps the cloven tongues experience, mentioned by Gee, was this occasion. Barratt returned to the Central Mission of Christiana (now Oslo) in Norway on December 1906 with the news of the gifts of the Spirit and his own personal experience.

As a result of his experience in America, revival attended his ministry wherever he went. This, undoubtedly, drew many people to his mission in Oslo seeking and curious. Barratt, though, felt he needed to be more free to spread the word of this latter day Pentecost so he resigned as *"... Superintendent of the 'Christiana City Mission'."*[161] (Barratt's italics) He then engaged in a lot of travel between 1908 - 1909[162] receiving invitations from many countries to go and share the full gospel message - Europe, India, Palestine and Syria. On his return to Norway in 1916 he founded the famous "Filadelfia Church" in Oslo which became the hub of Pentecostal revival in Europe for many years. It was rebuilt in magnificent style and re-opened in the centre of Oslo in 1938.[163]

Not everyone was enthusiastic about this new experience. The press, both secular and religious, had a great deal to say about it and much of it very critical. Barratt himself quotes from one such journal, *The Vanguard*, written by Baron Porcelli.[164] Barratt used this writing to show how ludicrous and illogical the charges were which were levelled against the new movement. Such criticism worked in the favour of Pentecostalism and fuelled the fire of curiosity causing many to come to see for themselves. Bloch-Hoell notes that it was such adverse publicity which helped to promote the rise of Pentecostalism in the beginning. [165] So who was this man and how did he influence Northern Europe so much with the Pentecostal message?[166]

Thomas Ball Barratt. (1862-1940) The contrast between Barratt and Seymour could not have been more marked, yet both of them were used in their own respective ways to bring the Pentecostal message to the world. It is probably fair to say they both had differing motivations and visions. Seymour's, as we have noted, was that of a social visionary, whilst Barratt's was that of a theological innovator.

Barratt was born in Albaston in Cornwall. His father was a mining engineer[167] whilst Seymour's was a slave. This implies that Barratt was from a middle class family or at least a family of means,[168] and he was white. William Kay notes that Barratt's family settled in Scandinavia due to his father accepting the position of a manager of a new mine in Norway, though he continued his education in Britain. Barratt spoke both English and Norwegian fluently.[169] He also had the privilege of further education in Norway. According to David Allen, Barratt studied art in Norway and music under the famous Norwegian composer Edvard Grieg. He says: "He was thus a man of considerable intellect and culture."[170] Allen also observes that Barratt's life was fairly uneventful until 1906 when he was forty-four.[171] His experience of the baptism in the Spirit in America changed his life forever. As a Methodist, Barratt was not unfamiliar with the concept of the baptism in the Spirit. Indeed Barratt gives a list of great preachers who "...had experienced it...." in his estimation.[172] Richard Massey confirms this saying Barratt wrote to Evan Roberts "...enquiring about 'a further baptism of fire'."[173]

Unlike Seymour, Barratt was an ordained minister of the Methodist Episcopal Church of Norway. Barratt had been preaching since a lad of seventeen and, according to Bloch-Hoell, it was he who actually founded the Oslo City Mission in 1902 and edited its newspaper -*Byposten*.[174] After his Spirit-baptism, Barratt felt called to take this message far and wide. His influence on Northern Europe is seen today in the numerous Pentecostal works, still existing, in most European countries. So how did it all come about?

The Scandinavian Explosion

Nils Bloch-Hoell, in his monumental work on the Pentecostal Movement, states that scholars universally acknowledge

Barratt "...as the apostle of the Pentecostal Movement in Europe."[175] It was Barratt's energy and zeal which created the interest and enthusiasm for this new move of God wherever he went. He did it through his preaching and literature - his books and particularly his magazine *Korsets Seier* (Victory of the Cross). As a Norwegian Methodist Episcopal he gained great prestige; his poise and integrity added to the spiritual stature of the man.

Norway. Barratt began his meetings in a large gymnasium[176] in Oslo but then sought a more permanent dwelling for his congregation. A.A. Boddy, the Anglican vicar from Sunderland who was to bring the Pentecostal movement to Britain, observes it was "...a mission room in an upper chamber. Perhaps about 120 people present."[177] It was here people, such as Boddy, came to from all over Europe as they had to Azusa Street. They came to investigate the Pentecostal revival taking place under Barratt. Press reports were the main source of advertising for Norwegian Pentecostalism. These reports, though not normally very supportive, served to create a curiosity within people from all quarters. They came from all over Northern Europe - Sweden, Denmark, Germany, England and Finland. Individuals, other than Barratt himself, went to various places with the Pentecostal message. In this way too Barratt influenced the spread of Pentecostalism either personally by word of mouth, through his literature or through the ministries of others.

From Barratt's church in Oslo the fire began to spread and Pentecostal assemblies began to emerge in Norway. Barratt says of his achievements in 1928: "...the assembly in 'Filadelfia' (the name of our hall), Oslo, is now the largest assembly of water and fire-baptised saints in Norway, and is the mother-assembly of many assemblies that have sprung up throughout the country."[178] The opening of his new and magnificent Filadelfia Church in Oslo in 1938 was a fitting tribute to the life and work of this honoured man of God.

Sweden. One such hungry soul who came to Oslo in 1907 was a young Baptist pastor from Sweden by the name of Lewi Pethrus. Bloch-Hoell says of the relationship between Pethrus and Barratt: "There is no doubt that the most outstanding personality of the Swedish Pentecostal Movement was won over to the movement by Barratt's example and instruction."[179] Through Pethrus many indigenous works sprung up in Sweden. However, as Bloch-Hoell also points out on the same page, Pethrus did not do it all on his own. Barratt also influenced others who came to Oslo from Sweden such as leaders within Swedish missions groups and Swedish Baptists as well as the editor of their periodical *Veckoposten*. Even though there is no certainty of their receiving the baptism in the Spirit in Oslo they returned with many favourable reports. They were Barratt's initial contacts in Sweden.

It was Pethrus though, who made the greatest impact. Formerly a Baptist pastor in Lidkoping and the Filadelfia Church, Stockholm, he was expelled from the Baptist movement in 1913 for, on the face of it, practicing open communion but in reality it was due to his Pentecostalism.[180] His famous Filadelfia Church, which was rebuilt to accommodate the huge crowds attending,[181] became a centre of Pentecostal excellence almost from the beginning. Through Pethrus a thriving programme of missions and outreach was introduced into the Swedish Pentecostal Movement. In this way Pethrus became the acknowledged leader of the Swedish Pentecostal churches with considerable influence throughout Europe.

Denmark. Bloch-Hoell says Barratt's "influence" can also be found in Denmark. Early in his ministry in Oslo, Danish interest was shown in what was going on through the many prayer requests Barratt was receiving from there. The key figures who brought the Pentecostal movement to prominence were all writers. The editor of *Kirkeklokken*, the Lutheran pastor H.J. Mygind and others, all wrote extensively about their experiences in Oslo. Press reports of the conversion to Pentecostalism of two famous actresses - Anna Larssen and Anna Lewini, also added to the advance of the Movement in Denmark.

Bloch-Hoell points out, however, it was not these people who actually brought the movement to Denmark but three Norwegians - a Mr Anthony, the editor of a magazine *Missionaeren* and two young ladies from Oslo. They did not, however, establish churches but influenced a small group of interested people from within the existing denominations and particularly the Lutheran Church. They also invited Barratt to come in 1908 to speak to this group and to which he returned. In this way Denmark was very different from other Scandinavian countries. Bloch-Hoell says: "...the interdenominational ideas of the early Pentecostal Movement were practised in these first years in Denmark."[182] He further suggests that this interdenominational emphasis and the existence of "... small groups not churches...."[183] kept the Pentecostal movement from formerly organising itself into a church. Although Barratt was keenly interested in such unity, the organisation of Pentecostalism as a distinct group happened after the Copenhagen Conference of 1919 as a consequence of disagreements within the ranks of Pentecostalism.[184]

Catalysts of the Spirit

Finland. Whilst Finns had been present in Oslo from the beginning and participated in the meetings, Barratt did not visit Finland until after the International Pentecostal Conference in Oslo in 1911. He had had numerous requests to visit from interested groups over the years but only accepted after the visit of some Finns to the Conference. This first visit did not result in setting up any organised church but contacts were made. One of the most notable, Bloch-Hoell says, was Pekka Brofeldt, editor of the Free Church paper *Toivon Tahti*. Barratt also established a monthly paper with articles from his own magazine *Korsets Seier* translated by Brofeldt. The one man credited with forming the Finns into a movement between 1919-1925 is G.O. Smidt. [185]

So then, by 1925 the Pentecostal movement, as an organised body of believers with a number of established churches, was firmly established in Scandinavia with Barratt as its undisputed apostle and spiritual father.

The European Invasion

As was said at the beginning, Barratt is regarded as the father of European Pentecostalism not simply Scandinavian Pentecostalism. Barratt influenced two other places *personally* - Germany and Britain - and possibly two others indirectly - Switzerland and France.

Germany. The main character in the advance of Pentecostalism in Germany is Jonathan Paul, whom Hollenweger describes as an: "...unassuming and learned theologian, against whom even his opponents have a high regard."[186] Hollenweger claims Paul had an earlier experience of sanctification through a vision.[187] So when he heard of the occurrences at Oslo he was naturally curious to see for himself. It seems he was convinced of the truth of the revival and, Bloch-Hoell says: "...acted as a spokesman for the Pentecostal Movement as early as the evangelistic conference in Brieg on 22-26 April 1907."[188]

Whilst Paul is regarded as one of its founders the real founders, according to Bloch-Hoell were two Norwegians - Dagmar Gregersen and Agnes Thelle who were brought to Hamburg by E. Meyer. These two ladies also influenced the evangelist Heinrich Dallmeyer who brought them to Kassel for meetings. Interest grew as a result of persecution and press coverage. Later support from Holland and England helped to further the cause. Barratt visited Germany twice in 1908 which no doubt strengthened the German leaders' cause. Some of his writings were also translated into German.

Southern Europe. The Swiss movement owes its beginnings, not to Barratt directly but to the two Norwegian ladies who also influenced the German movement. They arrived in Zurich 1907 and stayed for three weeks. They left a small group behind to continue the work. Barratt visited Zurich twice in 1908 and helped the little group to choose a leader. He had close contact with the Swiss church and followed its progress with interest. Bloch-Hoell informs us that: "In Holland and France the Norwegian Pentecostal Movement had a minimum of influence though '...Barratt had a proselyte in France in 1907.'"[189] His influence, however, did not reach far beyond there.

The British Connection

Another to visit Barratt in Norway was A.A. Boddy (1854-1930),[190] vicar of All Saints Church in Sunderland. Boddy was a man of great character and quality. Although he trained as a solicitor he entered the Anglican ministry and studied for a time under Bishop Lightfoot in Durham University.[191] On his ordination Lightfoot sent Boddy to a run down Parish in Sunderland, which he turned around with characteristic zeal. Boddy was a regular visitor at the Keswick Convention and took a keen interest in the

Welsh revivals occurring through Evan Roberts' ministry. It was these experiences no doubt which instilled in him the desire for revival. Sensing the excitement of revival in Barratt's church Boddy began seeking God for a new spiritual encounter. He claims to have received the baptism in the Spirit on March 5 1907 but did not speak in tongues until December 2 of the same year. [192]

After some pressure from Boddy, Barratt arrived in Sunderland from Norway at the end of August 1907. He commenced a series of meeting in the parish church which effectively lit the Pentecostal flame in Britain. What was intended as a brief visit became a prolonged stay. Barratt remained in Sunderland until October 18th 1907. All Saints rapidly came to be known as the spiritual centre of Britain. Seekers from every part of the country came to receive the baptism of the Holy Spirit with signs following. Boddy's means of promoting the movement was through the medium of his magazine *Confidence*[193] and his Whitsun Conventions. One such seeker at these Conventions was a humble plumber, Smith Wigglesworth (1859-1947), the leader of the Bowland Street Mission in Bradford. Wigglesworth was baptised in the Spirit when Mrs Boddy laid hands on him.[194] Wigglesworth was destined to become a renowned evangelist and one of the foremost leaders of the Pentecostal movement in

Britain through his extensive evangelistic campaigns. He is sometimes referred to as "The Apostle of Faith".[195] This is due to his amazing capacity to believe for the miraculous and to instil a similar faith in those who came to him for healing. Many miracles are said to have been seen at his meetings.

Like W. J. Seymour in Azusa Street., Boddy became a catalyst for the Pentecostal movement in Britain. Many seekers, who became household names in subsequent Pentecostal history, came to All Saints from all over and received their ministries through the Conventions at Sunderland. Like Seymour, Boddy also influenced others to become leaders in the British Pentecostal revival. In this sense Hollenweger is right when he calls Boddy, "The father of the British Pentecostal movement...." [196]

Cecil Polhill and the Pentecostal Missionary Union.[197]
Cecil Polhill (1860-1938) was one of the 'Cambridge Seven' athletes who had gone as missionaries to China in 1885.[198] Polhill had received the baptism in the Spirit in Los Angeles thus making another connection with Seymour and Azusa Street, though Gee says it was at a "...quiet meeting in a private house there."[199] Polhil's missionary drive and spirit brought to birth the Pentecostal Missionary Union or the PMU, as it was known. During its sixteen years the PMU sent out numerous men and women into

the mission fields to spread the message of Christ under the name of the emerging Pentecostal movement. It also produced such notables as W.F.P. Burton, George Jeffreys and E.J. Philips. The formation of this missionary agency showed the positive, forward-looking character of British Pentecostalism. There was no danger of it "...becoming a holy enclave..." according to William Kay.[200] At its heart was the desire to evangelise the world not just with the Pentecostal message but with the Christian gospel. The PMU eventually merged with Assemblies of God with the PMU as its missionary arm.[201]

The Jeffreys Brothers. On a visit to Sunderland in 1913 George Jeffreys (1889-1962) accepted an invitation from William Gillespie to visit Ireland.[202] It was there in 1915 that the Elim Evangelistic Band was formed. Through the efforts and influence of George and his brother Stephen, one of the largest Pentecostal Fellowships in Britain came into being - The Elim Pentecostal Churches or the Elim Foursquare Gospel Alliance to give them their official name.[203] George's strong, charismatic and authoritarian leadership was probably the main driving force in developing these churches along centralised lines akin to the Methodist Church government as the final authority rests with the Elim Conference. However, as Noel Brooks keenly points out, George was becoming increasingly uncomfortable with the encroaching "clericalism" creeping into Elim.[204] He began, Brooks claims, to argue for more lay involvement in the Elim Movement and it was this which caused the rift between George and Elim.[205] George broke away to form The Bible Pattern Church Fellowship but it never made much headway. Jeffreys' critics claimed he left because Elim would not adopt his British-Israelite beliefs. Brooks rejects this[206] as does Desmond Cartwright, official historian of the Elim Church. Cartwright claims the 'split' was more complicated than the issue of prophecy or church government. It was not simply the case of a man changing his mind on a point of theology but more a question of breakdowns in relationships. These breakdowns came about as a result of differences over the perceived scale of financial debt and its solution, together with George's failing health and his constant vacillations.[207]

Assemblies of God As a result of the Pentecostal ministry of people like Boddy many independent fellowships came into being. These independent assemblies began as an upshot of the Pentecostal experience in nominal churches and the evangelistic activities of the early Pentecostal pioneers who often planted new groups of Pentecostal believers. Other people who experienced the baptism in the Spirit had to leave the historic churches due to opposition.[208] They found themselves forced to meet together for ministry and fellowship. It soon became obvious that some form of standardised beliefs would have to be formulated but without infringing the independence of these local assemblies or making such beliefs a creed for salvation. It was on the 8th and 9th of May 1924, that Assemblies of God (AoG) came into being. According to Gee seven men were chosen as its first Executive Presbytery - Howard Carter, Thomas Myerscough, John Nelson Parr, Fred Watson, H.H. Webster, W. Davies and T.L. Hicks.[209] John Nelson Parr[210] became its first chairman, secretary and editor of the magazine *Redemption Tidings*. Assemblies of God had among their ranks notables like Donald Gee, Howard and John Carter and John Nelson Parr and pioneer missionaries such as W.F.P. Burton and James Salter, who founded the "Congo Evangelistic Mission".

The Apostolic Church Another Fellowship which arose out of this Pentecostal phenomenon was "The Apostolic Church". Indeed it may even be fair to say this was the first Pentecostal type church to arise in Britain as a result of the Pentecostal revival. The Apostolic Church was formed by the amalgamation of similar types of fellowships operating under the leadership of W.O. Hutchinson and his "Apostolic Faith Church" in

Bournemouth. Worsfold actually calls him the "...father of apostolic-type of Pentecostal movement in Great Britain."[211] It was reformed by Dan P. Williams and his brother W.J. Williams of Penygroes in Wales. In time the Penygroes group came to dominate and eventually a split occurred. Donald Gee states that it happened due to "...grave errors and extravagances...of the prophetic gift...and office of...apostle...."[212] Worsfold contests this, claiming it was over administration and finance adding: "...the differences which brought on the secession did not in any way involve doctrine."[213] Worsfold though suggests Welsh nationalism had a part to play in it all but this is highly contested. Gee may be more reliable here having been around at the time of the secession. Worsfold, as an Apostolic minister, may be allowing his bias to show through. In his defence, it has to be said, he does quote sources such as minutes and reports of the Apostolic Church.

Boddy had no direct influence on the formation of Pentecostal denominations, indeed he was probably against their formation as he saw the Pentecostal phenomena as a means of reviving the British church as a whole. Hollenweger says as much concerning Boddy and the Pentecostal movement: "He regarded it as a revival within the church and for this reason associated himself in 1909 with the Pentecostal Missionary Union, which was meant as a body within the Church."[214]

Conclusion

T.B. Barratt rightly deserves the title, Apostle of Europe, as it was through him that Pentecostalism came to the European continent. His influence was enormous and extensive. He promoted Pentecostalism through his writings, his magazine *Korsets Seier* and his various books. Speaking at many churches and Conferences also helped to propagate what was going on in Norway and other places. Yet it seems to me that he promoted the movement more through personal relationships than public appearances. He spent time with people such as Pethrus and Boddy and others to take the message out and personally encouraged them in their work. His major emphasis, it seems, was theological rather than social. This is seen in his opposition to W.H. Durham's 'two-stage' process of salvation – sanctification accompanying salvation. As a Wesleyan theologian Barratt held to the 'three-stage' process. Hollenweger quotes Barratt on this saying: "We do not accept the opinion of Durham, that all, in a moment in which they are born again, are wholly sanctified."[215] His books and literature are, in fact, a Pentecostal apologetic. The purpose of teaching the baptism in the Spirit, to Barratt, was to equip people for soul winning. In "A Friendly Talk to Ministers and Christian Workers" he constantly asks "...have souls been saved...?" or "...have bodies been healed...?" or the church "...cleansed..?"[216] Barratt's fundamental concern was for spiritual revival in the church leading to genuine unity but a unity based around the theological framework of Pentecostalism not a broad ecumenical creed. As he says himself:

> We pray earnestly that this movement may be accepted generally by all God's people. *Pentecost and its blessings, as well as Calvary, belong to ALL.* (italics Barratt's). Even if all Christians do not join the Pentecostal assemblies, churches and missions, that have sprung up during the last twenty years, and are constantly increasing in number, we still pray that this glorious revival of religion may enter churches and denominations, and clear out the debris of sin and formalism, and the false doctrines that have stopped their progress, and kindle the fire of Pentecost on their altars![217]

Barratt then was a pioneer in his own right, seeking to bring revival and renewal to the church as a whole. Like Seymour before him his ministry played a catalytic role in bringing Pentecostalism to the fore and releasing and equipping God's people to serve God's purposes more effectively. The Pentecostal movement in northern Europe is a lasting testimony to his success.

---

[155] R.M. Anderson, *Vision of the Disinherited* p105

[156] T.B. Barratt, (1927) *When the Fire Fell and an outline of my life*, Oslo.

[157] Allen, *The Unfailing Stream* p114

[158] D. William Faupel says two people communicated with him "Glenn Cook and May Throop" who were dealing with correspondence *The Everlasting Gospel* p22

[159] Gee, *The Pentecostal Movement* p15

[160] T.B. Barratt, *In The Days Of The Latter Rain* p144

[161] Barratt, *In The Days Of The latter Rain* p145

[162] Bloch-Hoell, *The Pentecostal Movement* p68

[163] Allen, *The Unfailing Stream* p115

[164] Barratt, *In The Days Of The latter Rain* p155. See also Gee *The Pentecostal Movement* p19 (c) and Bloch-Hoell *The Pentecostal Movement* p75,76

[165] Bloch-Hoell, *The Pentecostal Movement* p75

[166] Faupel says "Through Barratt's ministry, the Pentecostal movement was introduced to Norway, Sweden, Denmark, Germany, France, Switzerland and England." *The Everlasting Gospel* p221

[167] Massey, *Another Springtime* p18

[168] Anderson, *Vision of the Disinherited* p100

[169] William Kay, (1990) *Inside Story* Mattersey Hall Publishing,

Mattersey, England. p40.n10

[170] Allen, *The Unfailing Stream* p114

[171] Allen, *The Unfailing Stream* p115

[172] Barratt, *In The days Of The Latter Rain* p151

[173] Massey, *Another Springtime* p18

[174] Bloch-Hoell, *The Pentecostal Movement* p66

[175] Bloch-Hoell, *The Pentecostal Movement* p75

[176] P.D. Hocken, *Dictionary of Pentecostal and Charismatic Movements* p268

[177] Attributed to Alexander A Boddy by Kay, *The inside Story* p20

[178] Barratt, *In The Days Of The Latter Rain* p145

[179] Bloch-Hoell, *The Pentecostal Movement* p77

[180] Bloch-Hoell, *The Pentecostal Movement* p181

[181] Colin Whittaker, (1983) claims it seated 6,000 in 1921 *Seven Pentecostal Pioneers* Marshall, Morgan and Scott, Basingstoke, England p32

[182] Bloch-Hoell, *The Pentecostal Movement* p78

[183] Bloch-Hoell, *The Pentecostal Movement* p79

[184] Referred to by Bloch-Hoell in *The Pentecostal Movement* p79

[185] Bloch-Hoell, *The Pentecostal Movement* p85

[186] Hollenweger, *The Pentecostals* p237.

[187] Hollenweger, *The Pentecostals* p237.

[188] Bloch-Hoell, *The Pentecostal Movement* p79

[189] Bloch-Hoell, *The Pentecostal Movement* p86

[190] See Edith Blumhofer's article "Alexander Boddy and the Rise of Pentecostalism in Great Britain." *Pneuma: The Journal of the Society for Pentecostal Studies,* Spring 1986 pp31-40.

[191] Kay, *Inside Story* p17 Blumhofer, in her article, states that his bishop was Handley Moule "Alexander Boddy...." *Pneumatic: The Journal of the Society for Pentecostal Studies,* Spring 1986 p31

[192] Kay, *The Inside Story* p20

[193] A CDRom version of *Confidence* between 1908-1926 is available from Tony Gauchi, (2002) Revival Library, King's Centre, Bishop's Waltham, Hants. SO32 1AA. Tel. 01489 894734

Harry Letson

[194] This story is recounted in a letter Wigglesworth sent the Boddy in November 1907. Reprinted in Colin Whittaker, (1983) *Seven Pentecostal Pioneers,* Marshalls Paperbacks, Marshall, Morgan and Scott, Basingstoke, England. p26

[195] Title of the book by Stanley H. Frodsham *Smith Wigglesworth: Apostle of Faith Assemblies* of God Publishing House, Nottingham (1949 6th re print 1974)

[196] Hollenweger, The *Pentecostals p184*.

[197] John Andrews has written extensively on the missionary element in Pentecostalism in his unpublished PhD thesis entitled: *Regions Beyond*, University of Wales, Bangor. (2003)

[198] D.W. Bebbington, *Evangelicalism in Modern Britain* p197

[199] Gee, *The Pentecostal Movement* p48

[200] Kay, *The Inside Story* p58

[201] Whittaker, *Seven Pentecostal Pioneers* p115

[202] E. Boulton, (1928) *George Jeffreys - A Ministry of the Miraculous*, Elim Publishing House, London. p15

[203] Noel Brooks, *Fight for the Faith and Freedom,* published by The Pattern Bookroom (Notting Hill Gate, London undated). p36

[204] Brooks, *Fight for the Faith and Freedom* Ch IV "Clericalism"

[205] Brooks, *Fight for the Faith and Freedom* p43

[206] Brooks, *Fight for Faith and Freedom p74*-78 Hollenweger seems to confirm this *The Pentecostals* p199

[207] Desmond W. Cartwright, *The Great Evangelists*, Marshall Pickering, Basingstoke, England. (1986) p134&139. Cartwright deals with this issue at some length and is very informative.

[208] The Preamble to the *Constitutional Minutes of Assemblies of God* says that those who received the Pentecostal blessing wished to remain inside their respective fellowships but "Unfortunately their testimony all too often was opposed, and ultimately many believers... found themselves outside the existing churches...." p7

[209] Gee, *The Pentecostal Movement p129*

[210] See Henry Letson (2005) *Keeper of the Flame: The Story of John Nelson Parr*, unpublished PhD Thesis, University of Wales, Bangor. Ch 7.

[211] This is confirmed by J.E. Worsfold, *The Origins of the Apostolic Church in Great Britain,* Julian Literature Trust, Wellington, New Zealand (1991) p31

[212] Gee, *The Pentecostal Movement* p117

[213] Worsfold, *The Origins of the Apostolic Church in Great Britain* p152

[214] Hollenweger, The *Pentecostals* p185.

[215] Hollenweger, *The Pentecostals* p324.

[216] Barratt, (1928) *In The Days Of The latter Rain* Ch II Elim Publishing Co. London, England Ltd pp25-42

[217] Barratt, *In The Days Of The latter Rain* p221

Chapter 4: D. J. du Plessis: Catalyst of Unity

The burning desire at the heart of early Pentecostals was revival and a return to primitive Christianity and Christian unity. For this reason they were very much against formalism and organised Christianity which hindered unity. Their perception of unity was the unity of the Spirit based on Pentecostal principles. As Colin Dye pointed out at the joint Conference of Elim and Assemblies of God, unlike the term charismatic, Pentecostal was a doctrinal statement. Though many in the historic churches had received the Pentecostal experience their beliefs and practices have remained unchanged. For Dye, to be Pentecostal means to embrace all the doctrinal beliefs and theology associated with it. This is so on two counts.

Firstly, Pentecostals assert that they seek to restore New Testament beliefs, practices and experiences to the church. As previously mentioned, David A. Womack says: "We now use the word *Pentecostal* (Womack's italics) to mean the concept that there is one true Christianity that was taught by Jesus Christ and His followers... As Pentecostals we identify ourselves with the beliefs, experiences, practices and priorities of original, apostolic, New Testament Christianity."[218] This concept of unity among early Pentecostal was primarily a unity amongst Pentecostals as they had more to unite them than divide them. Gee's book *Toward Pentecostal Unity* implies this also.[219]

Secondly, it seems, the Pentecostal concept of unity was the church, as a whole, coming over to Pentecostal experience, theology and practice. This may sound a rather pretentious claim in this age of greater ecumenical engagement but for Dye and Womack Charismatic only refers to one aspect of Pentecostalism - the experience of the baptism and the gifts of the Holy Spirit.

Men like Seymour looked for a socio-ecumenical unity where all races, colours and creeds would become one in Christ,[220] and embrace Pentecostal experience and revelation. For Barratt too it seems it was a theological, spiritual unity but unity none the less. Yet within a short space of time Pentecostalism was falling into the very thing they protested against - sectarianism which fostered formalism, institutionalism and organisation.

It was this 'sectarian' attitude that brought about the formation of the various Pentecostal denominations, each one believing they were either re-defending New Testament principles or returning to them. P.G. Chappell affirms that this plethora of denominational growth occurred between 1907 and 1932.[221] D.B. Barrett claims there are now in existence "...11,000 Pentecostal denominations..." and "...3,000 independent charismatic denominations...."[222] Most Pentecostal denominations then were established during the period Chappell refers to. By denominations is meant specific groups, some with an administrative centre, holding similar beliefs and having a constitution or statement of faith.

Such fragmentation was not in the mind of men like Seymour, Barratt, Boddy and Gee who all had a bigger view of Pentecostalism and the Church at large. During the intervening time they and many others sought to bring unity among Pentecostals.[223] This, in fact, is what was behind the first Pentecostal World Conference in Zurich 4-9 May 1947. There had been various conferences in America and Europe but it was decided in Paris in 1946 that a Pentecostal World Conference should be set in motion and held every three years. The organising secretary for almost ten of those years, 1949-1958, was David J. du Plessis. This position in world Pentecostalism

Catalysts of the Spirit

gave Du Plessis the avenue of service he was destined to fulfil. Who was he and what was his contribution to Pentecostalism and the church at large?

David J. du Plessis (1905-87)

The shock wave of Azusa Street had a worldwide effect, reaching to many corners of the globe. One such place was South Africa. It was to here that Tom Hezmalhalch and John G. Lake came as missionaries in 1908 and established the Apostolic Faith Mission (AFM) of South Africa, built upon the foundation of Alexander Dowie's "Christian Catholic Church" which had been functioning in South Africa, since 1904.[224] In 1910 Hezmalhalch was elected as its first president. Spittler says that Hezmalhalch and Lake were actually missionaries from Dowie's church, in Illinois but "...had connections with the Azusa Street Mission."[225] Pentecostalism gained ground rapidly in South Africa, due in a large part to the Dutch Reformed Church and its strong Christian presence and tradition. The foundation laid by Andrew Murray and his teaching on the baptism in the Spirit and healing also aided its acceptance.[226] It was into this spiritual environment that David J. du Plessis was born.

Du Plessis was the oldest of nine sons. His parents, who had become Pentecostals through the work of Lake and

Hezmalhalch, were typically hardworking and industrious. His father was a carpenter and a lay preacher of solid Huguenot stock. While his father was a stern, strong man, his mother was gentle and sensitive.[227] In spite of this David was greatly devoted to his father whom he seems to have respected for his strength of character. It was this, no doubt, that put the steel in his own backbone, which he would need for his later work. He was converted in 1916, baptised in water 1917 and baptised in the Spirit in 1918 all within the Apostolic Faith Mission of Africa.

Although du Plessis attended colleges in Ladybrand and Bloemfontein[228] he had no formal theological training.[229] Irrespective of this he felt the call to ministry from his teens but was not ordained until the age of twenty-five in 1930. To begin with he served in a part time capacity until the opportunity opened for him to enter full time ministerial work. Within five years of his ordination he was to play an important role in the AFM. He edited their magazine *Trooster* meaning *Comforter*. A year later, 1936, he was elected as General Secretary, an office he held from 1936 to 1947. During his time he reorganised the Church's constitution, revised the magazine and opened an orphanage. He also had new offices built, purchased land for 'campground' and established a retirement fund for ministers based on a system of ministerial tithes.[230]

As can be seen Du Plessis's influence on the AFM and perhaps South Africa itself, was immense.

Du Plessis' destiny, however, lay not in South Africa but like John Wesley before him "The world was his parish." His destiny was made known to him it seems, through Smith Wigglesworth who reputedly gave him a prophecy. The substance of it was that du Plessis would witness, in his day, "...a revival that will eclipse anything we have known throughout history." All that was required of him was to be humble and faithful.[231] R.P. Spittler says this was referred to by du Plessis in a tract in 1951 but the full text of it was not printed until 1964.[232]

It was later, on a visit to America that it started to come to pass. Du Plessis together with Donald Gee and J.R. Flowers discussed Pentecostal unity and co-operation. It finally came to fruition in 1947 when the first Pentecostal World Conference (PWC) was convened in Zurich. Du Plessis was made organising secretary for the PWC, an office he held from 1949 to 1958. It was in this office that he found the fulfilment of the prophecy and his destiny. On his move to America he helped in the formation of the Pentecostal Fellowship of North America. He taught in a number of Colleges in spite of his lack of theological training. He spoke on the Far East Broadcasting Company, pastored two Assemblies of God Churches in Stamford and Dallas and served as Gordon Lindsay's organising secretary for "Voice of Healing Fellowship."[233] Strange as it may seem his destiny finally came into being through a car accident in Tennessee in 1949 when his car hit a stationary train in dense fog.[234] It was while he lay in his hospital bed that God began to unfold to him his future ministry. David Littlewood in Joy Magazine, comments: "He came out of hospital with his heart somehow changed...."[235] - softer and more open.

Du Plessis' new found ministry took him to many places and many people. It also took him into uncharted waters for a Pentecostal. It was in this that he made his greatest impact. Increasingly his feeling and desire for Christian unity prompted him to search out ways of touching other denominations and individuals. Du Plessis began reaching out to the ecumenical movement. True to his convictions he went into the offices of the World Council of Churches in New York City in 1949 and made himself known. Du Plessis was also led into the company of some very notable people engaged in ecumenical activity such as John Mackay, president of Princeton seminary. Mackay, according to Spittler, was "...du Plessis' gate into organised ecumenism."[236] Mackay asked him to speak at the International Missionary Council in Willigen, Germany in 1952. In this way du Plessis helped promote an atmosphere of change. He fostered a change of mentality in other denominations towards Pentecostalism and eventually some Pentecostals to other denominations. Du Plessis helped to create the space into which the Charismatic Movement could be born. In a sense he is seen as reversing the flow of the Spirit. Instead of expecting the Church universal to come to Pentecostals for the Spirit and his gifts, Du Plessis took the Spirit to them. No one would dare to suggest that David du Plessis created the Charismatic Movement, just as no one would attribute Pentecostalism to W.J. Seymour; they were merely catalysts and instruments of the Spirit. Like the Pentecostal outpouring before them, they built upon what was already happening in preceding generations and with courage and faith impelled it forward. Hocken asserts that du Plessis' contribution to the Charismatic Movement was to provide the "...vision of the Holy Spirit renewing the historic churches."[237] For many of his fellow Pentecostals this was an impossible task. Indeed, Andrew Walker claims, classical Pentecostals believed "...the older churches were apostate and incapable of genuine spiritual renewal."[238] What were the other forces at work then changing the face of Pentecostalism? Du Plessis certainly did not create them but, perhaps like Esther, he had *"...come to the kingdom for such a time as this."* (Esther 4:14)

Mass Evangelism

Alongside the growth of denominations was the growth of mass evangelism through crusades, the media (radio and eventually television) all with a literature backup of magazines and letters. These evangelists aided the growth of the Pentecostal movement by giving the Pentecostal experience a higher profile than ordinary Pentecostal church life and practice could. McClung, in his article, quotes Menzies as saying: "...the Pentecostal evangelists of the 1920s and 1930s had ministries that were far reaching in their influence." [239] They included the likes of Aimee Semple McPherson and Charles S. Price in America; Smith Wigglesworth and Stephen and George Jeffreys in Britain and T.B. Barratt and Lewi Pethrus on the continent. By and large, though, these early evangelists were associated with denominations, either in their founding or their establishment.

It was after the Second World War, that the so-called "healing evangelists" began to arise. This includes such figures as William Branham, Jack Coe, Oral Roberts, A.A. Allen, T.L.Osborne and Morris Cerullo.[240] With them mass evangelism entered a new phase; a phase which offered not only salvation and healing but wealth and prosperity as well. This paved the way for others such as Kenneth Hagin and Kenneth Copeland who was greatly influenced by

Hagin. These men - Hagin, Osborne and Copeland – it is claimed base much of their theology on E.W. Kenyon's teaching.[241] Generally speaking this new breed of evangelists had their own organisations, which stood independent of denominations, though some of them belonged to one Pentecostal denomination or another. In standing free from denominationalism these evangelists sought to involve all denominations, especially Pentecostal ones, in their crusades. In this way they crossed denominational barriers in order to bring their message to as many people as possible. However, P.D. Hocken notes: "By reaching across denominational lines and socio-economic levels, the healing revival gave birth to the modern charismatic movement in the late 1950s and 1960s."[242]

This interdenominational vision was given a further boost with the emergence of what came to be known as the Full Gospel Businessmen's organisation which gradually began to attract Catholics amongst its number to the consternation of classic Pentecostals.

The Full Gospel Businessmen's Fellowship International (FGBMFI)

The commencement of the FGBMFI was pioneered by Demos Shakarian in 1951.[243] It was intended as a gathering of unordained laymen coming together to simply share what God had done in their lives. Shakarian was encouraged in this venture by Oral Roberts. This indicates where Shakarian's commitment lay - the healing revival and cross-denominational co-operation. Shakarian drew largely on this independent sector of Pentecostalism to bring the message of healing and deliverance. Meeting in hotels and using 'laymen', sometimes Spirit-filled non-Pentecostals and in time Roman Catholic priests, caused many traditional Pentecostal ministers to remain aloof from the movement. The FGBMFI was yet another symptom of the diversification occurring within the Pentecostal family.

Such diversification within the ranks of Pentecostalism also caused further fragmentation. Many Pentecostals were deeply unhappy with the new breed of healing evangelists and FGBMFI. Their message seemed materialistic, worldly, and even Gnostic at times, and to add to the confusion - ecumenical. Many ministers from within and without the Pentecostal movement, refused to work with them. Yet the FGBMFI made a significant contribution to the rise of the Charismatic Movement within the church.

The Renewal Movements

With the help of du Plessis, the healing evangelists and FGBMFI, after the Second World War, the Pentecostal flame began to spread to the historic churches.[244] Many of the leaders in these churches began to feel they had been misguided in ignoring and ostracising Pentecostals. Among the Protestant denominations, ministers and people alike became more actively involved in seeking spiritual gifts. All this began to fuel the desire for "renewal" among the historic churches. Du Plessis was one of the leaders in the forefront of this new move. His contacts with the historic churches did much to make the Pentecostal experience accessible to them and earned him the title: "Mr Pentecost".[245] Donald Gee also dubbed him "a Pentecostal ambassador" saying he was "a man of God for the hour".[246] Gee supported him and his efforts all the way. Hocken says Gee "...provided intellectual grounds for positions du Plessis arrived at instinctively."[247] Both men, however, fell out of favour somewhat with their respective denominations for their efforts within the ecumenical movement. Du Plessis was actually disfellowshipped from American Assemblies of God in 1962[248] and Gee "...fell out of favour in America; he was replaced at Kenley."[249] Yet the prestige and standing of these two men undoubtedly furthered the cause of the Spirit among the traditional churches.

As a result of all this, people and ministers in traditional denominations began to look at the Pentecostal experience afresh. Many of them became more open to the things of the Spirit. Perhaps, too, T.B. Barratt's prayer was being answered when he said: "...we still pray that this glorious revival of religion may enter churches and denominations, and clear out the debris of sin and formalism, and the false doctrines that have stopped their progress, and kindle the fire of Pentecost on their altars!"[250]

Protestant Charismatics. This is what actually happened in the life of one Episcopalian minister, Dennis Bennett.[251] The beginnings of the Charismatic Renewal are usually traced to him and the public announcement to his Church - St Mark's, Van Nuys, California - Sunday 3rd April 1960. Bennett told them of his baptism in the Spirit and speaking in tongues. [252]

However, this was probably no more than a lot of ministers did after receiving the experience, so what was it that made Bennett so crucial? What gave it notoriety was publicity. The credit for this does not seem attributable to Bennett himself but to one of his congregation - Jean Stone. It was she who contacted two national journals, *Newsweek* and *Time*, concerning the events at Van Nuys. The publicity brought the charismatic activity of Bennett's church to the fore. Stone went on to publish her own magazine,

Trinity. These magazines together with the FGBMFI's magazine *Voice* were crucial elements in furthering the charismatic movement.[253]

Other ministers soon followed. In America, Lutherans like Larry and Evelyn Christenson, Presbyterians such as J. Rodman Williams and Harald Bredesen of the United Methodists to name a few. [254] In Britain, Anglicans like Michael Harper, David Watson and John Gunstone have led the way from the beginning. [255] Of the Baptists, David Pawson, Jim Graham, Paul Beasley-Murray and David Coffey are notables.[256]

To distinguish themselves from Pentecostals, Charismatics resorted to the use of the Greek word for spiritual gifts – "charismata". Thus the "Charismatic Renewal" was born. These people were not quite as definitive as the early Pentecostals concerning Pentecostal theology. Some believed in a second experience, others believed it to be no more than a revival of gifts which had been latent or dormant in the church. Most of them did not stress the 'initial evidence' of speaking in other tongues. [257]

Catholic Charismatics. The Charismatic Renewal soon spread to the Catholic Church. The "Catholic Charismatic Renewal" (CCR) is usually traced to a prayer meeting in Duquesne University, Pittsburgh in February 1967. It was helped in no small measure by the ecumenical trends of Vatican II (1962-65).[258] Nigel Scotland says it was through the influence of two books that the CCR came about. The books were David Wilkerson's *The Cross and the Switchblade* and John Sherrill's *They Speak with Other Tongues*.[259] Since that time it has grown to become an active force within Catholicism.[260] It has reached out particularly to Pentecostals with whom it has most in common. Notable figures over the years have been Kevin and Dorothy Ranaghan, Edward O'Connor and Kilian McDonnell. An important figure in bringing CCR to Europe was Cardinal Suenens of Belgium.

For many classical Pentecostals a sense of unease began to grow with CCR due to allegedly unwise and unbiblical statements emerging from the CCR. Statements asserting that the mass became more meaningful through speaking in tongues and that an understanding of Mary's role in salvation became clearer since being baptised in the Spirit. These were unwelcome to Pentecostals to say the least. Added to this was the increasing control of charismatic prayer meetings by the Catholic hierarchy causing many Pentecostals, myself included, to have grave doubts as we attended such meetings in Dublin and Belfast in the late seventies. [261] By the mid-seventies Pentecostal denominations came to be know as "classical Pentecostals" and both Catholics and Protestants from the historic churches as "Charismatics". This all emerged out of the so called "Neopentecostal" movement of the 1970s.

Du Plessis' main work then was in establishing Roman Catholic-Pentecostal dialogue. H.V. Synan observes that du Plessis was so valued by the Roman Catholic Church in this regard he received the "Gold Merit" medal from Pope John Paul II in 1983. He was the first non-Catholic to receive it.[262] Synan also links him with Cardinal Suenens in saying they were both "...destined to play major roles in the Catholic Charismatic renewal."[263]

Shepherding and Restorationism. To many Pentecostals and some Charismatics the Charismatic Renewal took a sinister turn in the Shepherding Movement. The leaders of this movement felt that many in the renewal movement had compromised basic truths of the kingdom, discipleship and the government of the church. Their great aim and desire was to see these things "restored" to the church. [264] Andrew Walker claims that the British version of Restoration did not originate in America though it was influenced by Christian Growth Ministries (CGM) and its leaders at Fort Lauderdale - Derek Prince, Bob Mumford, Charles Simpson, Don Basham, Ern Baxter and John

Poole.[265] Here in Britain it emerged through the ministry of Arthur Wallis, Bryn and Keri Jones, Terry Virgo and Gerald Coates and others. This movement owes much of its popularity and success to the writings of the late Arthur Wallis, a good and godly man of spiritual stature.[266]

Much of the success was also due to their magazine *Restoration* and the Dales Bible Weeks. Although their style of meeting and church service was very akin to Pentecostal services, their form of government is rather like the Apostolic Church. They demand commitment and submission from their adherents. This has exposed them to allegations of dictatorship, brainwashing and interference in the individual lives of their members. This teaching has caused much anxiety among Pentecostals and Charismatics alike. Hunter says it drew criticism from no less than du Plessis himself among others.[267]

Conclusion

Du Plessis' contribution to the Church at the end of the twentieth century is significant indeed. Like Seymour and Barratt before him he became a "catalyst"[268] in the cause of advancing the gospel of Christ. He suffered much from the barrage of criticism levelled against him. Yet his quiet strength and resolution won the day. Like his two great predecessors he fought for the unity of the Body of Christ. Though some may not agree with him and his love affair with ecumenism he has to be admired for his vision, courage, and tenacity. His obedience to what he believed to be the call of Christ also has to be applauded. If Seymour is seen as a "social visionary"[269] and Barratt a "theological innovator"[270] then du Plessis must be seen as an "ecumenical pathfinder".[271]

In spite of evangelical doubts surrounding ecumenism, du Plessis found a way of injecting new spiritual life into the whole proceedings through his teaching on the baptism in the Spirit and Pentecostal experience. In summing up du Plessis' contribution to the recent changes in the church at large R.P. Spittler says:

> Even apart from his leadership in the Roman Catholic-Pentecostal Dialogue, The PWC (Pentecostal World Conference), the charismatic movement as a whole, du Plessis' catalytic role affected a wide range of Pentecostal institutions: the Full Gospel Business Men's Fellowship International, Women's Aglow, the Pentecostal Fellowship of North America, and the Society for Pentecostal Studies.[272]

It remains to be seen how successful du Plessis has been in restoring spiritual life to the World Council of Churches to the satisfaction of all and what new spiritual directions the universal church, and particularly the evangelical wing, endeavours to take in order to be one that the world might believe - John 17:21. It has to be said uneasiness still exists within many Pentecostal circles over ecumenism and even the Charismatic Renewal and their potential to weaken and compromise the gospel as it is perceived by Pentecostals. Time alone will tell how things will pan out in the constant search for true unity in the church but for classical Pentecostals it still turns on their understanding of the gospel as it is expressed in Pentecostal hermeneutics.[273]

---

[218] Womack, *Pentecostal Experience: The Writings of Donald Gee* p13

[219] This has since been re-titled, according to Womack, to *All with One Accord* Gospel Publishing House, Springfield, Missouri, (1961) p224

[220] Dale T. Irvin, "Drawing All Together In one Bond of Love: The Ecumenical Vision of William J. Seymour and the Azusa Street Revival." *Journal of Pentecostal Theology* Issue 6 (1995)

[221] P.G. Chappell, "The Healing Movements" *Dictionary of Pentecostal and Charismatic Movements* p370

[222] D.B. Barrett, "Statistics" *Dictionary of Pentecostal and Charismatic Movements* p811

[223] Richard Massey, (1992) *Another Springtime*: Donald Gee,

Catalysts of the Spirit

Pentecostal Pioneer, A Biography, Highland Books, Guildford, Surrey, England. p144

[224] Hollenweger, *The Pentecostals* p120

[225] R.P. Spittler, *Dictionary of Pentecostal and Charismatic Movements* p250

[226] See Hollenweger, *The Pentecostals* pp111-116 for a fuller treatment of this.

[227] David du Plessis, (1977) *A Man Called Mr. Pentecost* as told to Bob Slosser, Logos International, Plainfield, N.J. p8,9

[228] David du Plessis, *A Man Called Mr. Pentecost* p63,64

[229] Hollenweger, *The Pentecostals* p7

[230] R.P. Spittler, "David Johannes du Plessis" *Dictionary of Pentecostal and Charismatic Movements* p252

[231] Colin Whittaker reprints this prophecy in full in his book *Seven Pentecostal Pioneers* pp40, 41 though he does not disclose his source.

[232] Spittler, *Dictionary of Pentecostal and Charismatic Movements* p251

[233] R.P. Spittler, *Dictionary of Pentecostal and Charismatic Movements* p252

[234] Du Plessis, *A Man Called Mr. Pentecost* p148

[235] D. Littlewood, "Mr. Pentecost: Sowing the Seeds of Worldwide Revival." *Joy Magazine* (May Edition 1997) Sheffield, England the official magazine of Assemblies of God in Gt. Britain and Ireland. p30

[236] Spittler, *Dictionary of Pentecostal and Charismatic Movements* p252

[237] P.D. Hocken, "Charismatic Movement" *Dictionary of Pentecostal and Charismatic Movements* p131 D.W. Faupel also claims that "... the influence of such men as David du Plessis and Oral Roberts laid the groundwork for this (cultural) breakthrough to take place." *The Everlasting Gospel* p15

[238] Andrew Walker, *The Blackwell Encyclopedia of Modern Christian Thought* Edited by Alister McGrath, Blackwell Publishers Inc.

Cambridge, Mass U.S.A. (1993) p430

[239] L.G. McClung Jr, "Evangelists" *Dictionary of Pentecostal and Charismatic Movements* p288

[240] H. V. Synan, (1984) *In the Latter Days,* Servant Books, Ann Arbor, Mich. USA p84,85

[241] See pp55ff of this book for a fuller explanation on this.

[242] P.D. Hocken, *Dictionary of Pentecostal and Charismatic Movements* p372

[243] See Synan p85, 86

[244] Hollenweger, *The Pentecostals* p6

[245] The title of his book: *A Man Called Mr. Pentecost* as told to Bob Sloss.

[246] Massey, *Another Springtime* p170

[247] Quoted in Massey, *Another Springtime* p172, 173

[248] Hollenweger, *The Pentecostals* p7

[249] Womack, *The Pentecostal Experience* p225

[250] Barratt, *In The days of The Latter Rain* p221

[251] Bennett, chronicles these events in his book *Nine O'clock in the Morning,* Kingsway Publications, Eastbourne, England (1970 last reprint 1981)

[252] Dennis Bennett, (1971 reprinted 1981) *Nine O'Clock in the Morning,* Kingsway Publications, Eastbourne, England. p8

[253] Nigel Scotland, (1995) *Charismatics and the Next Millennium: Do They Have a Future?* Hodder & Stoughton, London, Sydney and Auckland pp6,7

[254] P.D. Hocken, *Dictionary of Pentecostal and Charismatic Movements* p133, 134.

[255] John Gunstone, *Pentecost Comes to the Church* Ch 2 *Renewing Anglicans*.

[256] Scotland pp9,10 Peter Hocken gives a further list in his book *Streams of Renewal* pp110ff

[257] For the perspective of this as a second experience among Charismatics see J. Gunstone, *Pentecost Comes To The Church* Ch 3

"The Baptism in the Spirit." For the view that Spirit-baptism is not a second experience see Donald Bridges and David Phypers (1973, 1974) *Spiritual Gifts and the Church,* Inter-Varsity Press, London Section II "The baptism in the Spirit and spiritual gifts."

[258] Synan *In the Latter Days* p108. For a Catholic perspective see also Hocken, *The Strategy of the Spirit: Worldwide Renewal and Revival in the Established Church and Modern Movements,* Eagle Books, Guildford, England (1966) Ch 11 "Vatican II and after".

[259] Scotland, *Charismatics and the Next Millennium* p8

[260] Larry Christenson quotes the prayer of Pope John XXIII "Renew your wonders in our time as though for a new Pentecost..." as a sign of hope in the worldwide church - *A Message to the Charismatic Movement* Dimension Books, Bethany Fellowship Inc Minneapolis, U.S.A. (1972) p21

[261] D.D. Bundy makes reference to this concerning Suenens saying "...he decreed...only priests could lead prayer groups...." *Dictionary of Pentecostal and Charismatic Movements* p834

[262] Synan, *In the Latter Days* p88

[263] Synan, *In the Latter Days* p107

[264] D. Matthews, (1985) *Church Adrift* Marshalls Paperbacks, Marshall, Morgan and Scott, Basingstoke, England, pp163-165

[265] A. Walker, (1985) *Restoring the Kingdom* Hodder & Stoughton, London and other locations. p21

[266] Scotland, *Charismatics and the Next Millennium* pp10-13

[267] H.D. Hunter, *Dictionary of Pentecostal and Charismatic Movement* p784

[268] Synan, *In the Latter Days* p86

[269] See pp42ff of this book

[270] See pp90,91ff of this book

[271] Bunting, *Models of Ministry* Ch 4 "The Pathfinder"

[272] R.P Spittler, *Dictionary of Pentecostal and Charismatic Movement* p253

[273] See Gordon Fee, *God's Empowering Presence* and *Paul, the Spirit and the People of God.*

Conclusion:

Pentecostalism - Success or Failure?

Pentecostalism at the beginning of the twenty-first century has changed significantly from its humble beginnings at the turn of the twentieth century into a formidable force in the world. The question needs to be asked what Pentecostalism and its ministry really has achieved. For this reason I have sought to concentrate on three individual ministers who made a significant contribution to the growth and development of Pentecostalism. Looking back over the years can we say, with any degree of confidence, that the original objectives of these founding fathers have been achieved? In order to do this of course we need to specify what these original objectives were and to what extent their vision has been fulfilled.

Reviving the Church. In the days preceding Azusa Street, aspirations of holiness and revival of true religion seemed to go hand in hand.[274] Edith Blumhofer suggests British Pentecostalism inherited all the hopes and dreams of revival from Keswick and the Welsh revival.[275] Pentecostalism in Great Britain of course was the natural recipient but so also was Azusa Street in Los Angeles, the birth place of Pentecostalism.[276] Indeed Faupel contends that Pentecostalism "As a system of thought...had been in gestation for over half a century."[277] Aspirations after holiness and the purification of the church were believed to precede a great revival which would sweep away all dead and sterile religion. It was also believed that this great revival would unify the church and all true believers in preparation for the second coming of Christ. Hollenweger encapsulates the whole thing in saying: "A Pentecostal pastor knows that he is the servant of the final age of revival, which has returned to the earth in the days before the end."[278]

The connection between holiness, revival and eschatology is very clear in Pentecostal theology. Pentecostal ministers, traditionally, see themselves as calling people to prepare for the coming of the Lord Jesus by repentance and holiness of life. The baptism in the Spirit is seen as an aid in empowering God's people to unify and evangelise in the light of the soon coming of Christ. Faupel puts it succinctly: "The adherents understood the presence of unknown tongues to mean that a second day of Pentecost had been poured out which would empower them to announce the last great message of warning to a dying world and a sleeping church."[279]

Arguably, Pentecostalism has revived the Church at large in many respects. It has enlivened its worship, advanced the cause of missions alongside a growing social awareness and fostered the desire for genuine, spiritual unity.

Liberating the Laity. This great revival in the Church would not only purify it and draw others into it but it would do so through the release of the so called laity.[280] Fee shows clearly that leadership emerges from amongst the people of God themselves by the power of the Holy Spirit.[281] It is this which prompted me to define the model in the Introduction.[282] In it I sought to show the Spirit at the centre, and working outward, empowering and equipping the people of God for service through the ministry of its leaders. This liberation of individual members is one of the most successful aspects of Pentecostalism. Harvey Cox describes Seymour as "...presiding over this gentle pandemonium with tact and...personal diplomacy." He goes on to describe the meeting in Azusa Street saying those attending "...sat facing each other. People spoke from anywhere, but for those who felt especially anointed, the shoebox pulpit was generously open to anyone."[283] This liberating tendency within Pentecostalism is generally acknowledged from Walter Hollenweger in 1969 speaking of "The rediscovery of the laity in the church",[284] to John Gunstone, former County Ecumenical Officer of Greater Manchester, in 1994 addressing the issue of "Every Member Ministries".[285]

Breaking the Barriers. Early Pentecostal ministers saw the message of Pentecost as God's way of breaking the barriers of sin, sickness, demonism and social injustice through the power of the Spirit, evidenced in speaking in tongues. To them it was God's way of reviving the church and replacing the crippling effects of formalism and ritualism in the church with real, living Christianity. These early pioneers seemed to stand outside the church as a whole and challenge and beckon people to come to them for the truth. Barratt puts it thus: "And this Pentecostal Movement is too great to be bound by any single denomination or sect. It works outside and gathers all together in ties of love...." He goes on to say: "We do not fight against persons or church denominations, but endeavour to displace dead forms and confessions and wild fanaticisms with living practical Christianity."[286]

However it was not merely religious or spiritual barriers these early ministers sought to break but social ones as well. This comes out clearly in the life of W.J. Seymour.

Seymour also firmly believed that the Pentecostal revival would bring an end to all racial and social divisions.[287] R. M. Anderson sees the rise of Pentecostalism as "... one small part of a widespread, long-term protest against the whole thrust of modern urban-industrial capitalist society."[288] D. Petersen says much the same thing but within a Latin American 'Liberation Theology' context.[289] Admittedly, these perspectives on Pentecostal origins may be called into question but they at least show the potential for dynamic social change within Pentecostalism.

This opinion, though, seems to have been a recent development. It begs the question as to whether someone like Seymour could go along with such an interpretation. Certainly Barratt, du Plessis and Gee would be hard pressed to fit the Pentecostal movement into such a socio-political mould. They were primarily spiritual leaders whose only aim was to revive the church and evangelise the lost. That this social praxis may have been the outcome of Pentecostalism liberating the laity is one thing but to suggest it was the whole purpose or a hidden agenda seems to stretch the point to me. However it must be admitted that Pentecostalism has brought release to people in all levels of society and it looks set to continue to do so for the future.

Looking into the mists of the twenty-first century we need to ask where Pentecostalism is going. With the rise of ecumenism and cross-denominational co-operation great changes seem to be afoot. As a result of the Charismatic Movement, the more traditional Pentecostals and others are expressing the concern that Pentecostals are compromising the truth.[290] The immortal words of Spock to Captain James T. Kirk of the "Starship Enterprise" could aptly be applied to the Pentecostal movement at the beginning of the twenty-first century – "It's life Jim but not as we know it!" Pentecostalism has changed drastically and dramatically in some cases. In some ways it has changed beyond recognition. Pentecostalism, at the beginning of this new millennium bears very little resemblance to the holiness roots from whence it came. It appears now to be an amalgam of diverse beliefs and practices. It contains classical Pentecostals, Protestants and Catholic Charismatics and Restorationists as well as the controversial "health and wealth" preachers who have been within its ranks from the beginning.

The Third Wave

Yet other changes have taken place into a third move or a "Third Wave"[291] as C. Peter Wagner calls it. [292] To Wagner, Pentecostalism is moving into a new level of consciousness; a third level. It appears similar to the first two but with a number of significant differences. Classical Pentecostalism was the first wave and the Charismatic movement the second. John Wimber says a similar thing in his book *Power Evangelism* when he speaks of "The Next Stage."[293] These new breeds of Christians do not want to be identified with either Pentecostals or Charismatics.[294] Firstly, they reject the baptism in the Spirit as a second experience instead they make it simultaneous with salvation. Secondly, they believe in multiple fillings with the Spirit without the sign of tongues. Thirdly, they believe in the gifts of the Spirit under the power and anointing of the Spirit as an aid to evangelism.[295] Fourthly, their overriding emphasis, according to Harvey Cox, is that of demonism.[296] According to Third Wave, demonic forces rule all levels of human society Cox says. He shows this to be so as a result of the success of Frank Peretti's book *This Present Darkness*. Rather than a novel or piece of "whimsical" Christian literature like C.S. Lewis' *Screwtape Letters*, Cox sees it in a more worrying and sinister light. For Cox "...metaphor had somehow become metaphysic, a story had turned to an ideology."[297]

Is this then where Pentecostalism is going? Wagner infers that this third wave emerged out of the church growth seminars in Fuller School of World Missions. In this sense it began with John Wimber and his course on signs and wonders theology.[298] Much of this work is woven into Wimber's book: *Power Evangelism*. However, it is all still in its formative stages. It is too early yet to see whether or not it will have the impact or lasting effect of the previous "two waves". Andrew Walker says though it might be "...a useful analytical distinction." To try to break Pentecostalism down into three or four waves is not a neat one.[299]

The Toronto Experience

On the back of all this another new wave in 1994, or perhaps a harbinger of the Third Wave in some ways, in what has come to be known as the Toronto Blessing. People were claiming a fresh touch of the Spirit and experiencing renewal. Much laughter, falling down and excitement has been reported. People, it is said, were being saved, healed and cleansed. Others claimed God had healed various kinds of relationships in marriage and families. The down side was the criticism of much excess. People were reported to be "barking like dogs", running around with their arms outstretched as though flying like a plane or an eagle. Others were said to be swimming or crawling backwards under the chairs.

That the Toronto Experience was being identified with John Wimber and Third Wave theology comes out very plainly in writers advocating it. Mike Fearon for one clearly shows this in his book *A Breath of Fresh Air*.[300] Chapter four of this book is actually entitled "Riding on the Third Wave."

Many Christians and theologians see the present spiritual movement as God's way of renewing and unifying the church. For many Christians alive today it is seen as the most exciting period in Church History; the last great revival preparing God's people for the coming of Christ. However, it must also be said that others see it as New Age coming into the church; a sign of the last great apostasy. This too is associated with the Second Coming but in a pejorative sense. We should not shrink from hearing hard and apparently threatening criticism from scholars such as Dave Hunt and T. A. McMahon who have been very scathing in their comments. Their warnings and criticisms of the new developments in Christianity and particularly Pentecostalism require an answer. They see much of the recent spiritual phenomena as paving the way for the antichrist and the one world church. They criticise such people as Paul (now known as David) Yonggi Cho, Richard Foster, John Wimber, Francis McNutt, Dennis and Rita Bennett, Agnes Sandford, Robert L. Wise, Ruth

Carter Stapleton, Robert Schuller, Kenneth Copeland and Kenneth Hagin to name a few, as propagating a deception.[301] Most of these are involved in the Pentecostal and Charismatic Renewal. They accuse them of using New Age language and mind manipulation techniques and term it as "The seductive gospel of selfism...."[302] According to Hunt and McMahon this is nothing more than shamanism and transcendentalism reformed into what came to be known as "New Thought" which has "....survived on the fringes of the church in extreme Pentecostalism...."[303] Such New Age practices, they say, are "...the 'great delusion' that will sweep the world in 'the last days' and cause humanity to worship antichrist."[304] Such a diverse interpretation of the Pentecostal and Charismatic movement causes great pain in many genuine and sincere Pentecostal believers. Yet it is fair to say they make a crucial point which must be dealt with.

Whilst keeping their warnings in mind, it seems to me we need to have more faith in the words of the Saviour who promised to build his church - the "Gates of Hades" would never overcome it - Matt 16:18. There is something in this new air of optimism in the Church which fills me with excitement. Perhaps some of the vision hopes and dreams of our early pioneers in seeing salvation, social justice and healing may yet come to fruition. In spite of the worrying trends there are signs of hope. Pentecostalism is becoming more open, self-critical and subjecting itself to scholarly investigation and dialogue and responding to it all with some relish. Perhaps the hopes and dreams of Seymour, Barratt and Du Plessis are nearing their fulfilment after all.

Summary

Pentecostalism has been at the forefront of all the plans and purposes of God for his world. Individual ministers of the movement have been the catalysts of the Spirit to bring about great change not only in the church but in the world in general. They have highlighted the power and might of God through their emphasis on the miraculous. They have helped release the vast army of ordinary men and women, often referred to as the laity by the established churches, empowering them through the Holy Spirit. They have energised and motivated others to bring new hope for the poor and dispossessed particularly in the Third World, as well as the hope of reconciliation within the Church itself that we may know the true unity for which Jesus prayed. Finally, the great outpouring of the Spirit in the Twentieth Century has reminded us that God is ultimately in charge of his creation and that one

Catalysts of the Spirit

day, perhaps not too far off, Jesus will come again to make all things new as God intended.

---

[274] David W. Bebbington, (1989) *Evangelicalism in Modern Britain* pp161-165

[275] Blumhofer "Alexander Boddy" *Pneuma* 8:1 (Spring, 1986) p31

[276] Faupel mentions the visit of F.B. Meyer "...an exponent of Keswick...." to Los Angeles in 1905 and Meyer's telling people of the great Welsh revival occurring under Evan Roberts. This prompted Joseph Smale of the First Baptist Church to go to Wales to see for himself. *The Everlasting Gospel.* p193. However, some recent studies indicate that Smale went to Wales for reasons of health. Perhaps then his visit had a twofold purpose.

[277] Faupel, *The Everlasting Gospel* p44, 45.

[278] Hollenweger, *The Pentecostals* p413

[279] Faupel, *The Everlasting Gospel* p 307

[280] See the three models outlined in the Introduction pp 1,2,3

[281] G.D. Fee, *Gospel and Spirit* p131

[282] See p3ff of this book

[283] Cox, *Fire from Heaven* p57

[284] Hollenweger, *The Pentecostals* p244

[285] Gunstone, *Pentecost Comes to the Church* p73ff

[286] Quoted in Bloch-Hoell, *The Pentecostal Movement* p46

[287] See this book p62ff

[288] R.M. Anderson, *Vision of the Disinherited* p223

[289] D. Petersen, *Not by Might nor by Power* Ch 5 &6

[290] V. Budgen, *Charismatics and the Word of God : A biblical and historical perspective on the charismatic movement,* Evangelical Press, Welwyn, England (1985)

[291] C.P. Wagner, *Dictionary of Pentecostal and Charismatic Movements* p843-844 see also D.B. Barrett *Dictionary of Pentecostal and Charismatic Movements pp820*-829 for a fuller explanation of the Three Waves concept.

[292] G.B. McGee, *Dictionary of Pentecostal and Charismatic Movements* p875

[293] John Wimber with Kevin Springer, (1985 4th Print 1986) *Power Evangelism: Signs and Wonders Today Hodder*, Stoughton, London and other locations Ch 8.

[294] Peter Wagner is quoted as saying just this in Wimber's book *Power Evangelism* p131 "I see myself as neither a charismatic nor a Pentecostal. I belong to Lake Avenue Congregational Church. I'm a Congregationalist. My church is not a charismatic church, although some of our members are charismatic."

[295] This is the thrust and import of Wimber's book: *Power Evangelism*

[296] Cox, *Fire From Heaven* p281-287

[297] Cox, *Fire From Heaven* p285

[298] C.P. Wagner, *Dictionary of Pentecostal and Charismatic Movements* p889

[299] Andrew Walker, "Pentecostalism and charismatic Christianity" *Encyclopedia of Modern Thought* p433

[300] Mike Fearon, (1994) *A Breath of Fresh Air*, Eagle, an imprint of Inter Publishing Services (IPS), Guildford, Surrey, England.

[301] D. Hunt and T.A. McMahon, *The Seduction of Christianity*, Harvest House Publishers, Eugene, Oregon, U.S.A. (1985) p193

[302] Hunt and McMahon, *The Seduction of Christianity* p193

[303] Hunt and McMahon, *The Seduction of Christianity* p151

[304] Hunt and McMahon, *The Seduction of Christianity* p7

BIBLIOGRAPHY

Books and Booklets

Allen, D. (1994) *The Unfailing Stream* Sovereign World, Tonbridge, England.

Anderson, Robert M. (1979) *Vision of the Disinherited: The Making of American Pentecostalism*, Oxford University Press, Oxford and New York.

Barratt, T.B. (1909, 1928) *In The Days of the Latter Rain* Elim Publishing Co., Ltd.

Bartleman, F. (1980) *Azusa St: The Roots of Modern-Day Pentecost* Logos International Plainfield, N.J.

Bennett, D. (1981) *Nine O'Clock in the Morning* Kingsway Publications, East Bourne, England

Bloch-Hoell, N. (1964) *The Pentecostal Movement: It Origin, Development and Distinctive Character* Universtetforlaget, Oslo and Allen and Unwin London.

Blumhofer, E. (1993) *Restoring the Faith: The Assemblies of God, Pentecostalism and American Culture*, University of Ilinois Press, Urbana and Chicago.

Blumhofer, E. (1989) *The Assemblies of God: A Chapter in the Story of American Pentecostalism* - 2 Volumes, Gospel Publishing House, Springfield, Miss.

Boardman, W.E. (1860) *The Higher Christian Life* James Nisbet and Co. London.

Bocock, R. and Thompson, K. (1985) *Religion and Ideology* Manchester University Press in Association with The Open University, Manchester, England.

Boulton, E. C.W. (1928) *George Jeffreys - A Ministry of the Miraculous*, Elim Publishing House, London

Boyd G. A (1992) *Oneness Pentecostals and the Trinity* Baker Book House, Grand Rapids, Mich.. U.S.A

Brierley, P. (1991) *Christian England: What the Church Census Reveals, Marc* Europe, London, England

Brewster P.S. (1976) Editor *Pentecostal Doctrine,* Printed by Grenehurst Press, Cheltenham, England.

Bridges D. and Phypers D. (1973,1974) *Spiritual Gifts and the Church* Inter-Varsity Press, London

Brooks, N. (undated) *Fight for the Faith and Freedom* published by The Pattern Bookroom Notting Hill Gate, London.

Brumback C. (1959) *God in Three Persons* Pathway Press, Cleveland, Te, U.S.A

Brumback, C. (1961) *Suddenly from Heaven: A History of Assemblies of God* Gospel Publishing House, Springfield, Missouri

Bunting, Ian (1993, 1996) *Models of Ministry: Managing the Church Today* Grove Books Ltd, Cambridge, (1993, 1996)

Burton, W. (1956) *Signs Following* Elim Publishing Co., Ltd. London, England.

Carter, H. (undated) *Questions and Answers on Spiritual Gifts* Harrison House Inc. Tulsa, Ok. U.S.A. in Cooperation with the Assemblies of God Publishing House, Nottingham, England.

Carter, J. (1979) *A Full Life: The autobiography of a Pentecostal Pioneer* Printed by Evangel Press, London

Cartwright, D. W. (1986) *The Great Evangelists* Marshall Pickering, Basingstoke, England.

Cook, Philip L. (1996) *Zion City, Illinois: Twentieth-Century Utopia*, Syracuse University Press, New York, USA.

Cox, H. (1996) *Fire from Heaven* Cassell London

Dayton Donald W (1987) Theological Roots of Pentecostalism Zondervan Publishers, Grand Rapids, Michigan. USA

Edwards, Jonathan. (1965) *Selected Work of Jonathan Edwards Volume 1* Banner of Truth Trust. London. Containing: *A Narrative of Surprising Conversions* (1736) *The Distinguishing Marks of a Work of God* (1741) and An Account of the Revival in Northampton 1740-1742 (unpublished letter) and Sermons.

Faupel, D.W. (1996) *The Everlasting Gospel: The Significance of Eschatology in the Development of Pentecostal*

Thought Sheffield Academic Press, Sheffield, England

Fee G.D. (1994, 1995) *The Empowering Presence of God: The Holy Spirit in the Letters of Paul* Hendrickson Publishers, Inc Peabody, Mass. U.S.A.

Fee G.D. (1991, 1994) *Gospel and Spirit: Issues in New Testament Hermeneutics* Hendrickson Publishers Inc, Peasbody, Mass. U.S.A

Finney, C.G. (last reprint 1973) *Power From On High* Victory Press, East Bourne, Sussex

Frodsham, S. H. (1949 6th re print 1974) *Smith Wigglesworth: Apostle of Faith* Assemblies of God Publishing House, Nottingham

Gee, D. (1st published 1930 last edition 1952) *Concerning Shepherds and Sheepfolds: A Series of Studies Dealing With Pastors and Assemblies,* Elim Publishing House, London, England.

Gee, D. (Preface dated 1928) *Concerning Spiritual Gifts,* Gospel Publishing House, Springfield, Missouri, U.S.A.

Gee, D. (1941) *The Pentecostal Movement* Victory Press, London

Gee D (1980) *These Men I knew* Assemblies of God Publishing House, Nottingham. England

Goff, J. R. (1988) *Fields White Unto Harvest: Charles F.*

Parham and the Missionary Origins of Pentecostalism by. Fayetteville, AR: University of Arkansas Press.

Gunstone, J. (1994) *Pentecost Comes to Church: Sacraments and Spiritual Gifts,* Darton, Longman and Todd, London.

Hacking, W. (1981 formerly *Reminiscences of Smith Wigglesworth* published 1972) *Smith Wigglesworth Remembered* Harrison House, Tulsa, Oklahoma, U.S.A

Harvey, V.C. (1964) *A Handbook of Theological Terms,* Samuel Bagster and Sons Ltd. London.

Hollenweger, W. J. (1972) *The Pentecostals* SCM Press, London

Hollenweger, W. J. (1997) *Pentecostalism: Origins and developments worldwide.* Hendrickson, Peabody, Mass.

Horton, H. (Undated) *Arrows of Deliverance* Assemblies of God Publishing House, London.

Jeffreys, G. (1933) *Pentecostal Rays: The Baptism and Gifts of the Holy Spirit,* Elim Publishing Co. Ltd. London, England

Jeffreys, E. (1946) *Stephen Jeffreys: The Beloved Evangelist,* Elim Publishing Co. Ltd. London.

Kay W. K. (1990) *Inside Story* Mattersey Hall Publishing. Mattersey, England.

Kay W.K. (2000) *Pentecostals in Britain* Paternoster Press, Carlisle, England

Lancaster, J. (1973) *The Spirit-Filled Church,* Grenehurst Press, Cheltenham, England.

Massey, R. (1992) *Another Springtime: Donald Gee Pentecostal Pioneer,* Highland Books, Guildford, Surrey.

Matthews, D. (1985) *Church Adrift: Where in the world are we going?* Marshalls Paperbacks, Marshall, Morgan and Scott, Basingstoke, England.

Missen, A. F. (1973) *The Sound of a Going* Assemblies of God Publishing House, Nottingham, England.

Mauro P. (reprint 1974) *The Gospel of the Kingdom: An Examination of Dispensationalism* Reiner Publications, Swengel, PA. U.S.A

Neighbour R.W. (1990) *Where Do We Go From Here?* Touch Publications, Houston. Texas. USA

Newbigin, Lesslie (1954) *The Household of God* Friendship Press, New York.

Parr, John Nelson (1972) *"Incredible!" Autobiography of John Nelson Parr.* Privately published and distributed by the author and later by Marjorie Parr. Copyright Fleetwood March.

Parsons, G. (1988) *Religion in Victorian England Vol 1*

Traditions Manchester University Press, Manchester and New York, In Association With The Open University.

Petersen, D. (1996) *Not by Might Nor By Power: A Pentecostal Theology of Social Concern in Latin America.* Regnum Books International, Paternoster Press, Carlisle England.

Randal, Ian. (1999) *Evangelical Experiences: A Study in the Spirituality of English Evangelicalism1918-1939* Paternoster Press, Carlisle, England

Richardson, W.T.H. (1972) *Pentecost is Dynamite* Lakeland, Blundell House, London

Riggs M.R. (1948) *The Spirit-Filled Pastor's Guide,* Gospel Publishing House, Springfield, Missouri, U.S.A.

Robeck, Cecil M (2006) *Azusa Street Mission and Revival: The Birth of the Global Pentecostal Movement*, Thomas Nelson, Nashville, Tennessee. USA.

Scotland Nigel, (1995) *Charismatics and the Next Millennium: Do They Have a Future?* Hodder & Stoughton, London, Sydney and Auckland.

Samuel L. (1962 and 1964) *Evangelicals and the Ecumenical Movement,* The Evangelical Alliance, London England.

Snyder H.A. (1977) *The Community of the King,* Inter-Varsity Press, Downers Grove, Illinois. U.S.A.

Synan H.V. (1971) *The Holiness-Pentecostal Church in the United States*, William B. Eerdmans Publishing House, Grand Rapids, Mich. USA.

Synan H.V. (1984) *In the Latter Days: The Outpouring of the Holy Spirit in the Twentieth Century,* Servant Books, Ann Arbour, Mich.

Valdez Sr A.C. (1980) *Fire on Azusa St: An Eye-Witness Account* Gift Publication, Costa Mesa California.

Various Authors (1970) *Church Doctrine and Practice,* published by The Precious Seed Committee

Virgo T. (1985) *Restoration in the Church,* Kingsway Publications, Eastbourne, England

Goff Jr. R and Wacker Grant, (Editors) (2002) *Portraits of a Generation: Early Pentecostal Leaders*, University of Kansas Press, Fayetteville, Kansas. USA

Wagner C.P. (1973) *Look out! The Pentecostals Are Coming,* Coverdale House Publishers, London and Eastbourne, England

Walker, A. (1985) *Restoring the Kingdom* Hodder and Stoughton, London and other locations.

Walker, Williston (1970) *A History of the Christian Church* by (Third Edition) T&T Clark. Edinburgh.

Walvoord J.F. (1978 12th edition) *The Millennial Kingdom*

Zondervan Publishing House, Michigan, U.S.A.

Warrington, Keith. Editor (1998) *Pentecostal Perspectives* Paternoster Press Carlisle.

Watson, Thomas. (1692, 1970) *A Body of Divinity* The Banner of Truth Trust. London. England.

Whittaker, C. (1984 revised 1990) *Great Revivals* Marshall Pickering/Collins Publishing Group London, England and other location.

Whittaker, C. (1983) *Seven Pentecostal Pioneers* Marshall, Morgan and Scott, Basingstoke, England.

Wigglesworth, S. (1995) *Faith That Prevails* Radiant Books, Gospel Publishing House, Springfield, Missouri, U.S.A.

Williams, J.R. (1992) *Renewal Theology: Systematic Theology from a Charismatic Perspective, 3 Volumes* Zondervan Publishing House, Grand Rapids, Michigan.

Wimber J. with K. Springer (1985 4th Print 1986) *Power Evangelism: Signs and Wonders Today* Hodder and Stoughton, London and other locations .

Wood, A.R. (1969) *Evangelistic Sermon Outlines* Kregel Publications, Grand Rapids, Michigan USA

Womack, D.A. (1993) Complier & Editor *Pentecostal Experience: The Writings of Donald Gee* Gospel Publishing House, Springfield, Missouri.

Womack, D.A. (1968) *Well-Springs of the Pentecostal Movement* Gospel Publishing House, Springfield, Missouri.

Worsfold, J.E. (1991) *The Origins of the Apostolic Church in Great Britain,* Julian Literature Trust, Wellington, New Zealand

Dictionaries and Encyclopaedias

Dictionary of Pentecostal and Charismatic Movements (1996 9th edition) Editors Burgess, S.M. and McGee, B.G. Zondervan Publishing House Grand Rapids Michigan

Encyclopaedia Britannica (1992), London and other locations, 15th Edition Vol. 8

Expository Dictionary of New Testament Words by W.E. Vine, Oliphants, Marshall, Morgan and Scott, London, England. (First published 1940 this edition 1978)

New Dictionary of Christian Ethics and Pastoral Theology (1995) Editors: Atkinson, D. J. and Field, D.H. Inter-Varsity Leicester, England and Downers Grove Illinois, U.S.A

New Dictionary of Theology (1988) Editors: Ferguson, S. B. and Wright, D. F. Inter-Varsity Press, Leicester, England and Downers Grove, Illinois U.S.A.

The Blackwell Encyclopedia of Modern Christian Thought (1993) Editor: McGrath, A. Blackwell Publishers Inc. Cambridge, Mass U.S.A.

Webster's Third New International Dictionary (1971) *Encyclopaedia Britannica, Inc.* Chicago and other locations. G&C Merriam Co.

The New Dictionary of Christian Ethics and Pastoral Theology (1995) Intervarsity Press, Leicester England and Downers Grove, Illinois, USA

The Penguin Dictionary of Sociology (1984 and 1988) Editors: Abercrombie, N. Hill, S. and Turner, B.S. Penguin Books, London, England, New York, U.S.A. and Victoria, Australia.

Journals and Magazines

Believers Voice of Victory Vol. 22 No. 12 December 1994 pp18-21and Vol 23 No. 4 April 1995 p12-14 & 19 Bath, England.

Journal of Pentecostal Theology (1995) Issue 6 Church of God School of Theology, Cleveland, U.S.A

The Spirit & Church Gospel Theological Seminary, Taejon City. South Korea. Vol 3 No 1 May 2001 John McKay "Pentecost and History"

Pneuma: The Journal for the Society for Pentecostal Studies Vol 15, No 1, Spring 1993 P.O. Box 2671 Gaithersburg, MD 20886 USA.

Journal of European Pentecostal Theological Association

Editor Keith Warrington Published by EPTA, Natwich Cheshire 2002

Joy Magazine, Sheffield, England the official magazine of Assemblies of God in Gt. Britain and Ireland.

Themelios Vol 20, 3 May 199538 De Montford St. Leicester, England.

Theology [SPCK Journal of Theology] March/April 1995 and May/June 1996

Joy Magazine, Sheffield, England the official magazine of Assemblies of God in Gt. Britain and Ireland.

Theses and Dissertations

Allen, D. (1990) *Signs and Wonders: The Origins, Growth, Development and Significance of Assemblies of God in Great Britain and Ireland.* Unpublished PhD thesis University of London.

Andrews, John. (2003) *Regions Beyond,* unpublished PhD thesis, University of Wales, Bangor.

Hocken P. *Baptised in the Spirit: The Origins of the Charismatic Movement in Great Britain,* unpublished PhD thesis University of Birmingham. 1984

Kay, William. (1989) *A History of Assemblies of God* unpublished PhD thesis, University of Nottingham.

Letson, Henry. (1997) *Pentecostal Ministry: Its History and Influence*, unpublished Masters thesis, University of Wales, Cardiff.

Letson, Henry. (2005) *Keeper of the Flame: The Story of John Nelson Parr*, unpublished PhD thesis, University of Wales, Bangor.

Massey, Richard. (1987) A *Sound and Scriptural Union: An Examination of the Origins of Assemblies of God in Great Britain and Ireland during the years 1920-1925*, unpublished PhD thesis university of Birmingham.

Nelson, D. J. (1981) *For Such A Time As This: The Story of Bishop W.J. Seymour*, unpublished PhD thesis, University of Birmingham, England.

Petts D. (1993) *Healing and the Atonement*, unpublished PhD thesis, University of Nottingham

Randall, I. (1997) *Movements of Evangelical Spirituality in the Inter-war England*, unpublished PhD thesis, University of Wales, Cardiff.

Taylor, M. J. (1994) *Publish and Be Blessed: A Case Study of Early Pentecostal Publishing History, unpublished* Ph.D. thesis University of Birmingham

P.C. Software and Internet

Williams J.R. www.home.regents.edu/rodwil/ **A Theological Pilgrimage** *Chapters 7, 11, 14, 15*

Confidence Published by Tony Cauchi on CD-Rom, Revival Library, King's Centre, High St. Bishops Waltham, Hants, SO32 1AA

Lion PC Bible Handbook, *History of Christianity,* Lion PC Handbook (1993, 1994)